Frank Lloyd Wright and Le Corbusier

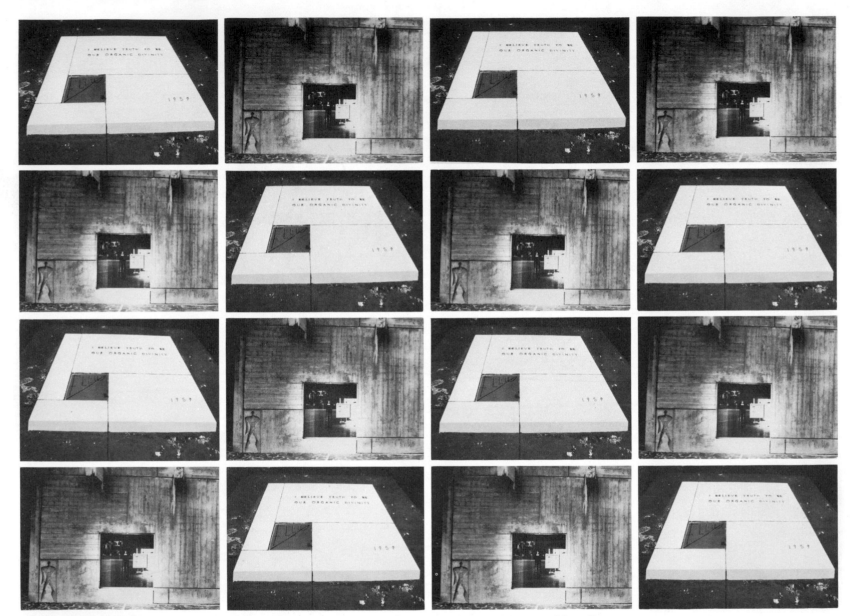

Wright: Frank Lloyd Wright Memorial, Florida Southern College.   Le Corbusier: Unité d'Habitation, Marseilles.

Frank Lloyd Wright and Le Corbusier

The Great Dialogue

Thomas Doremus

VNR VAN NOSTRAND REINHOLD COMPANY
New York

To Adolf K. Placzek

Printed in the United States of America
Designed by Sharen DuGoff Egana

Published by Van Nostrand Reinhold Company Inc.
135 West 50th Street
New York, New York 10020

Van Nostrand Reinhold Company Limited
Molly Millars Lane
Wokingham, Berkshire RG11 2PY, England

Van Nostrand Reinhold
480 La Trobe Street
Melbourne, Victoria 3000, Australia

Macmillan of Canada
Division of Canada Publishing Corporation
164 Commander Boulevard
Agincourt, Ontario M1S 3C7, Canada

16 15 14 13 12 11 10 9 8 7 6 5 4 3 2 1

Library of Congress Cataloging in Publication Data
Doremus, Thomas, 1946–
  Frank Lloyd Wright and Le Corbusier.

  Bibliography: p. 187
  Includes index.
  1. Wright, Frank Lloyd, 1867–1959. 2. Le Corbusier, 1887–
1965. 3. Architectural criticism. 4. Architecture—Philosophy.
I. Title.
NA737.W7D67 1985   720'.92'4   84-20952
ISBN 0-442-21837-0

What name, what skill, what faith hast thou in things!
What sight in searching the most antique springs!
What weight and what authority in thy speech!
Man scarce can make that doubt, but thou canst teach.
Pardon free truth and let thy modesty,
Which conquers all, be once overcome by thee.
Many of thine, this better could than I;
But for their powers, accept my piety.

—Ben Jonson, 1616

vulnerable. Only by surrendering to the most basic of spatial impulses—the fear of falling represented by the pull of gravity down the ramp—can one gradually regain control of one's spatial perception. This experience, so marked in criticism on the building, is unique in architecture.

It is not hard to find a similar experiment in a late project of Le Corbusier, that for the French Embassy in Brasilia of 1964 (fig. 8-3b). Le Corbusier understood as well as Wright did that a Modern space could be created by superimposing the radial order of a circle upon the bidirectionality of a square. For the Secretariat of the Embassy, he proposed that the circular perimeter wall contain a cubic interior based on a Cartesian grid. It can be anticipated from his plans and models that the space would have strongly suggested a central axis at the circular perimeter but a Cartesian grid at the rectangularly ordered center. Moving around in the space would be an experience of shifting plan types, a withholding or "erasing" of the expected central axis.

This experience is reversed at Le Corbusier's Carpenter Center for the Visual Arts at Harvard University, built between 1961 and 1964. Here, it is the achievement of the order of a Cartesian grid that is withheld. The grid is sensed upon approach, buried within the curved masses that spring out from the core. As at the Guggenheim, a ramp is the main circulation device, curving at first but finally aligning itself with the grid (figs. 8-4a, b). It passes through the Cartesian continuum, allowing angled motion independent of the grid itself to reinforce the integrity of the Cartesian system. The transparency of the generated planes is, as at the Guggenheim, the result of displaying contradictory perceptual cues.

Thus, the Carpenter Center, like the Guggenheim Museum, evokes a transcendental multiplicity of space

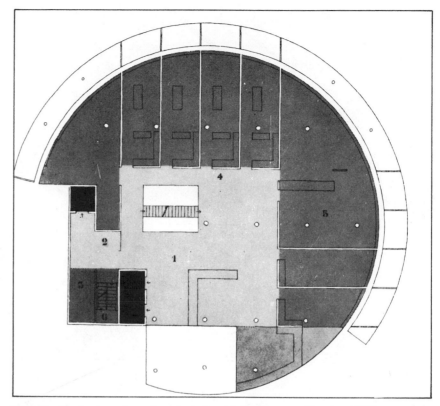

8-3b. Le Corbusier: plan of project, French Embassy at Brasilia, 1964. (Courtesy of Fondation Le Corbusier.)

8-4a. Wright: Guggenheim Museum.

8-4b. Le Corbusier: Carpenter Center, Harvard University, 1961.

8-5a. Wright: Guggenheim Museum.

(figs. 8-5a, b). This, of course, brings up the third characteristic of Modern form: *disjuncture*. The melange of free-form curves and straight planes at the street level of the Carpenter Center is gradually resolved vertically into a straightforward cubic mass at the upper levels. The path to order, then, is upward at the Carpenter Center and downward at the Guggenheim. Again, the Carpenter Center's homogeneous surface rendering and clearly resolved edges contribute to the reading of the intersecting forms.

A much simpler building is Wright's Buckner Library of 1941 at Florida Southern College (figs. 8-6a, b). The two functional areas—reading room and stacks—are given circular and hexagonal geometries, respectively. The floating mass of the stacks is contrasted with the strongly expressed radial beams supporting the circular roof of the reading room, weaving in and out of the roof planes and screen wall. Since early plans for the Guggenheim suggested a variety of hexagonal and circular schemes, all of Wright's circular and angular plans of the 1940s and 1950s can be examined as experiments leading to the Guggenheim Museum.

It is clear that underlying the three characteristics of Modern form discussed above is multiplicity, the interaction of independent coordinated systems. The fourth characteristic—*dynamic balance*—refers both to this and to dynamism, the other determinant of Modernism. The intensified dynamism of the Guggenheim Museum, represented by the harnessing of the force of gravity to the architectural continuum, was anticipated by Wright in the Morris Gift Shop of 1948 in San Francisco. Here, Wright establishes with utmost simplicity the archetypal configuration of urban street architecture: a plain brick screen wall in alignment with adjoining facades. The penetration of this screen is something that has been previously associated with the International Style, particularly in Le Corbusier's Villa Stein at Garches. The Organic approach is usually less direct. But Wright uses the act of penetration to make a statement about the response of a virtual system, represented by the wall, to human interaction. The arched entry is off-center, a circumstance in the generalized plane of brick. But the arching of the brick, a comment on Classical attitudes toward construction, is denied inside the entrance tunnel, where the angled brick arches are stopped at midpoint by curved sheets of glass. The glass doors at the end of this tunnel seem to have been pushed through the brick, which fractures in response to the force of entry (fig. 8-7a). The intersection of the semicylindrical entrance tunnel and the cubic interior of the shop is disjoined from the intersection of brick and glass. The system of materials is left independent of the geometric system of the plan. This is a dynamic configuration, a representation of systems not in ordered hierarchy but in interaction. The dynamic is continued, of course, with the spiral ramp, set off-center to the rectangle of the floor plan. Thus, the movement of the open plan is reinforced by the comprehension of spaces determined by interacting forces, by displaced axes and materials breaking and forming in response to each other.

Very similar in its establishment of coordinated dynamic interaction is Le Corbusier's pavilion at Zurich, designed as a residence planned to incorporate some display function in 1964–65, but finally built as a small gallery after Le Corbusier's death. Here, a virtual transparent plane is established by the continuous vertical edge of the elements of the metal canopy. The entrance tunnel is cubic rather than cylindrical, a rectangular space half penetrating the paneled wall of the house and half reaching out past the house but still beneath the canopy (fig. 8-

8-5b. Le Corbusier: Carpenter Center.

8-6a. Wright: Buckner Library, Florida Southern College, Lakeland, 1941.

8-6b. Le Corbusier: Carpenter Center.

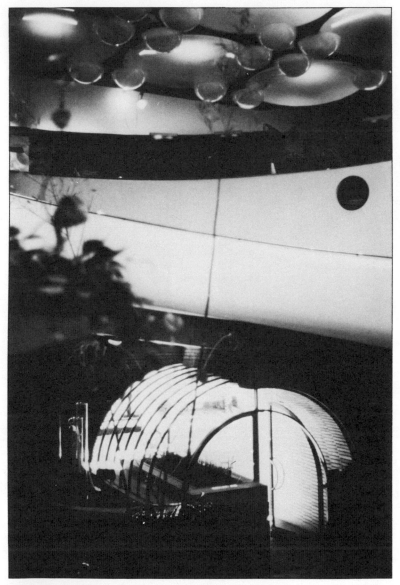

8-7a. Wright: Morris Gift Shop, San Francisco, 1948.
(Courtesy of Fredric Rosen.)

7b). In plan, the canopy is a double square, reinforced by the opposing bends of the twin roofs. The house itself is a smaller double square, but broken and pushed to different corners of the larger two squares by the act of entry and vertical circulation, just like the dynamic effect of circulation on the plan of the Morris shop. Again, entry is off-center, circumstantial and not unlike, in its circuitous progression, Wright's typical entrance sequence in the Prairie houses. The use of ramps in both buildings makes the act of circulation a dynamic experience.

For the fifth and final characteristic of Modern form—*definition of parts within systems through clear articulation*—two quite special houses will be examined. Wright's Friedman House of 1948 at Pleasantville, New York, has many of the characteristics of the classic Prairie house. Two intersecting volumes, one taller than the other, define the basic *parti*. Stone walls break free from the house itself and reach out to the surrounding site to define a natural domain (fig. 8-8a). There is a central fireplace, and even the inverted Palladian windows of the living room control the view with their rhythmic scoops into the masonry. But Wright's late geometry is used instead of the foursquare Prairie plan. Two intersecting cones, one diminishing downward and the other diminishing upward, as at the Guggenheim, form the interpenetration of the principal masses. The smooth poured concrete of the polygonal roof discs is clearly separated from the rough masonry of the walls by window bands. In fact, the independence of the canopies from the walls, exactly the situation at the Zurich Pavilion, is explicit at the approach drive where a freestanding concrete umbrella forms a later version of the Wrightian porte cochere. The windows are defined by red-painted frames and impose their rhythm on the rough stone walls in the living room, but depend on the radial plan drawn in the red-

8-7b. Le Corbusier: Zurich Pavilion, Zurich, 1964. (Courtesy of Fondation Le Corbusier.)

8-8a. Wright: Friedman House, Pleasantville, New York, 1948.

8-8b. Le Corbusier: Villa Shodhan, Ahmedabad, 1955. (© Retoria/Y. Futagawa & Associated Photographers.)

8-9. Wright: Friedman House.

painted concrete floor slab (fig. 8-9). Even the reinforcing of the poured concrete roofs is briefly revealed in a red-painted steel I-beam crossing the gap carved from the lower canopy by the penetrating second floor balcony above the living room. This, of course, is directly analogous to the wooden tracery stretching free of its stucco infill where the library balcony interpenetrates the living room of the Baker House.

This lucid expression of interacting systems is also present at Le Corbusier's Villa Shodhan, built in India in the early 1950s. Here, the Cartesian space of his 1920s houses is exploded into its culminating manifestation. Each of the five sides of the cubic house—four elevations and roof—is a composite of screen walls, window panels, *brise-soleil* recesses, and structural web edges (fig. 8-8b). The adjustment of formwork patterns allows each element to be completely readable at the same time that the homogeneously rendered surface strongly expresses the

continuity of the enclosing material, responding variously to functional and environmental requirements. Just as Wright abandoned his overly lush detailing for a straightforward exposure of major building systems, Le Corbusier replaced the thin and tenuous detailing of his early houses with a more plastic and substantial treatment of articulation.

It is evident from the above that what is constant between the early and late careers of the two architects, as far as formal analysis goes, is also common between them. As was discovered earlier, distinctions between Wright and Le Corbusier are most important in the areas of technology and iconography, and even these distinctions are of far less significance than the similarities, most of all in form and, as shall now be confirmed, function.

For exploring the Modern attitude toward function in the later careers of Wright and Le Corbusier, the most complex and problematic functional type that either of them ever had a chance at, the governmental center, will be examined, namely Wright's Marin County Civic Center and Le Corbusier's capitol complex at Chandigarh. Particular problems arise with this comparison. Wright's program was a great deal more restricted than Le Corbusier's in that he was dealing with the regional administrative center of an established local community with clear programmatic aims. Le Corbusier, however, had much more of a clean slate since the local culture was not only alien to him but, to a great extent, idealized for him by the attitudes and motives of those responsible for dreaming up the project in the first place. It can be expected, therefore, that a greater emphasis on dramatizing the functions of government will be apparent in Chandigarh. Then again, the Marin County Civic Center was one of the last buildings on Wright's drawing board before he died and the final design and construction supervision were finished by his successors at Taliesin. Nevertheless, its importance in Wright's oeuvre is undeniable.

As far as criticism of Wright's work is concerned, the Marin County Civic Center has been probably the stickiest thorn in the side of the architectural press. Never was his work more at odds with the fashion of the times, its delicacy and refinement of detail and glowing color flying smack in the face of the heroic brutalism and International Style revivalism of the early 1960s. It might even be proposed that the building was one of the most important determinants in sealing critical vision against all of Wright's late work. But a willingness to take an unprejudiced look, a sincere surrender to the authority of Wright's unparalleled experience, will result in a perception of the comprehensiveness and lucidity of the Civic Center and, ultimately, his entire oeuvre.

Wright had visited Italy in the 1950s and had been impressed enough with the arcuated architecture of Roman aqueducts and Renaissance palazzi to call for arches upon visiting the site of the proposed building. His final product managed to combine the plastic and monumental qualities of Mediterranean building with the sophistication of that quintessential civic center, the Doge's Palace in Venice. Thus, the huge entrance arches of the ground-level wings of the building progress vertically through stages to circular perforations in a thin shell of concrete, magically transforming the massive concrete base into a tightly stretched fabric at the top floor (fig. 8-10a). The wings of the building imply both cave and tent, swelling upward as if in response to the billowing space within.

At the Palace of Justice at Chandigarh, there is also an arched entry portal formed by the tall, rain-catching parasol roof (fig. 8-10b). But where Wright's double roofs are split to catch light, Le Corbusier's are split to form a channel that conducts rainwater

to spouts at the ends of the building. Both buildings have roofs shaped to environmental phenomena; each responds according to local needs. But Le Corbusier provides roof terraces as refuge from the harsh local climate, whereas Wright leads each of his floors directly out to hillside terraces at the ends of each wing for maximum accessibility to the mild climate of Marin County.

Examining the layouts of the administrative and judicial wings of the Marin County Civic Center, one finds that they are similar to those of the Secretariat and Hall of Justice buildings, respectively, at Chandigarh (figs. 8-11a, b). Both the Secretariat and Marin County administrative wing are long, narrow slabs, simply supported on quadruple rows of columns and containing office space on either side of central corridors. Both buildings offer private access corridor/balconies outboard of the offices with brise-soleil-type screens. The comparison can even be extended to the decorative metal handrails, a pattern of intersecting circles in Wright's building and free-form bent steel rails in Le Corbusier's Secretariat and Hall of Justice. Both administrative buildings have vertical circulation cores dispersed rhythmically throughout; these include minor connections to the outside at ground level, as well as major entrances beneath grand portals that penetrate the wings laterally. Wright's entrance is designed for the automobile traffic of northern California, whereas Le Corbusier depresses his automobile access below grade.

The judicial wings are similarly laid out, too. Rows of courtrooms have public and private access separated on either side. Judges' offices are behind and above the courtrooms. Both architects tried to diminish the intimidating quality commonly associated with courtrooms, Wright by bringing the major participants into a circular arrangement of similar desks

8-10a. Wright: Marin County Civic Center, San Rafael, 1957. (Courtesy of Nancy Monroe.)

8-10b. Le Corbusier: Palace of Justice, Chandigarh, 1952–56. (Courtesy of E. Teitelman/Photography.)

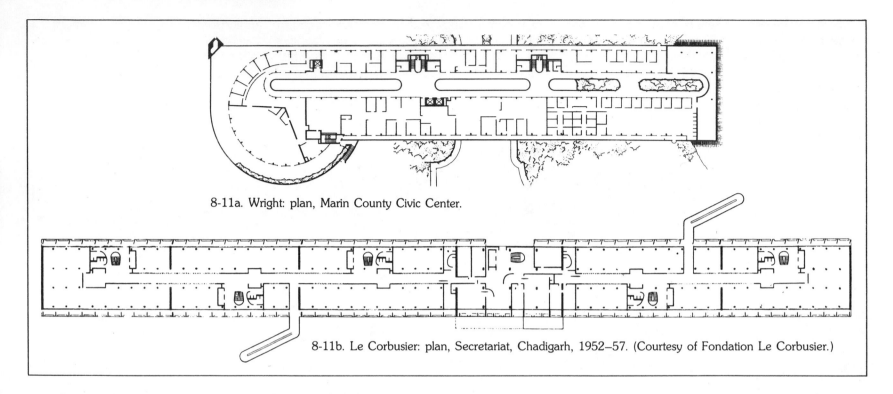

8-11a. Wright: plan, Marin County Civic Center.

8-11b. Le Corbusier: plan, Secretariat, Chadigarh, 1952–57. (Courtesy of Fondation Le Corbusier.)

and Le Corbusier by covering the walls with decorative tapestries, demonstrating their common desire to stress the administrative side of the judicial presence over the punitive.

With this overview, the first of the two aspects of function, *function as use,* can be discussed. In terms of responsiveness, the functional layout of the two complexes, each tailored to specific uses, has already been mentioned. Wright chooses a different shape, a domed cylinder, for his library, a center for learning that he saw as more important than the administrative or even judicial activities of the county government (fig. 8-12a). Reminiscent of his circular library at Florida Southern College, its

reading room gives importance to the citizen/user over the functions of government. Le Corbusier chooses a similar contrasting shape, the hyperbolic cylinder, for his Assembly building at Chandigarh (fig. 8-12b). The administrative wings of this building are wrapped around the Assembly Room cylinder like the cloister of La Tourette rather than the straightforward slabs of the Secretariat and Hall of Justice. Noteworthy, too, is the off-center placement of this cylinder in the rectangular plan of the building, recalling Wright's similar configuration in the Morris Gift Shop.

Flexibility can be found in the loftlike office spaces of both administrative buildings and in the modular, repetitive nature of both sets of courtrooms. A complex section in all three buildings allows for double-height ministers' offices and courtrooms at Chandigarh and a hidden jail in Wright's Hall of Justice.

The other aspect of function in Modern architecture is *function as purpose*. The functional types developed by both Wright and Le Corbusier have been discussed. In their later careers, certain of these types appear to have been switched between the two. It might be said, for example, that the longitudinal blocks of space represented by the Robie House reappear in Le Corbusier's late version of his own Catalan vault-type house, the Maisons Jaoul, built in Paris in the early 1950s. Correspondence is not just limited to the similarity in materials, systems, and structure but can also be discerned in the manner in which the main living floor of House B is divided by a stairwell and freestanding fireplace like those of the Robie House. The grass-covered roofs, initiated by Le Corbusier in the 1920s, appear in some of Wright's berm-type houses of the 1940s and 1950s.

Characteristic of their later careers is the precision with which prototypical (relating to function) and archetypical (relating to structure) images are expressed. Le Corbusier's Zurich Pavilion explicitly separates the prototypical sheltering canopy from the archetypical assemblage of industrial systems that compose the cave-and-tent house beneath. The detailing—bolted steel angles for the structural frame, modular opaque and glazed infill panels for the skin, industrialized stair construction—reinforces the collage of independent systems that give resonance to the multiple imagery. Wright's Anderton Court Shops of 1952 in Beverly Hills, California, simultaneously express a variation on his tent archetype and a spiral ramp version of his cloister prototype for observing items on display (fig. 8-13). The concrete "tent posts" seem to stretch webs of glass between them,

a reading supported by the overlapping of angled glass planes and the typically late-Wrightian detailing of metal mullions in such a way that the mullions fall independent of the actual joints in the glass (fig. 8-14). It is as if the independent systems that make a tent possible—the poles, wires, and fabric—are transmutated into the concrete, metal, and glass at Anderton Court. The spiral cloister prototype is used here in conjunction with Wright's tent archetype, whereas at the Morris Gift Shop in San Francisco and at the Guggenheim Museum, the spiral is used together with his sky-cave archetype.

The umbrella-roof configuration has already been pointed out in Wright's Friedman House and Florida Southern College as well as in Le Corbusier's Zurich Pavilion and capitol at Chandigarh. But a distinction should be made in both architects' work between two prototypical configurations for a space. One is the sidelit sheltering roof, developed first as the *parti* of the Prairie house and continued by Wright throughout his career, primarily in residential buildings. Le Corbusier's umbrella roof prototype is in most respects identical to this. The other is the toplit, closed-sided space, dubbed the "sky-cave," developed by Wright in the Larkin Building and Unity Temple, and later used frequently in his public buildings, such as the Johnson Wax Headquarters, the Guggenheim Museum, the Beth Sholom Synagogue, and the Annie Pfeiffer Chapel at Florida Southern College. Le Corbusier first developed this configuration in his houses, culminating at the Villa Savoie with its protective enframing walls around the open roof terraces. He explored it in a more Wrightian manner in his late churches and most spectacularly at the Assembly Chamber at Chandigarh. If these two configurations may be called the *shelter* and the *cloister,* respectively, it is clear that in final form, the cave-and-tent archetypes de-

8-12a. Wright: Marin County Civic Center. (Courtesy of Nancy Monroe.)

8-12b. Le Corbusier: Assembly, Chandigarh, 1952. (Courtesy of E. Teitelman/Photography.)

8-13. Wright: Anderton Court Shops, Beverly Hills, 1952.   8-14. Wright: Anderton Court Shops.

veloped by both architects are always used in conjunction with one or both of these two prototypes. For both men, the shelter implies a moderate protection from the natural environment and encourages an open social interaction among users. The cloister is used in situations of either personal or communal contemplation or concentration on a particular task, such as in a workplace or church. Although certainly not exclusive to the work of Wright and Le Corbusier, it is significant that these two prototypical configurations appear to be explicit in their work and to have been recognized and adopted by such architects as Aalto and Kahn.

Having established the basic similarities in the formal and functional aspects of Wright's and Le Corbusier's late work, the discussion may proceed to areas where more important distinctions arise, the technical and the iconographic.

The first characteristic of the technical in Modern architecture is *expression of structure*. Wright's response to the post-and-beam system of the International Style has already been discussed at length. But an increasing suavity can be discerned in the way he develops his structure in relation to the other building systems. The ultimate example, once again, is the Guggenheim Museum, where the formal, functional, and structural influences on the building are so thoroughly integrated as to appear seamless, yet each can still be traced clearly through the building on its own. Wright intensified the integrity of the component systems of his late buildings at the same time as he increased their interaction. At the Beth Sholom Synagogue, a tour de force of tenuous reinforced-concrete framing members, the fenestration system is allowed to retain its basic perpendicular configuration of joints, but whole walls of it are tilted in response to the angled concrete supports and even overlap each other, resulting in the patterns

of superimposed grids that are one of the central esthetic themes of the synagogue. But Wright's primary interest was in reinforced concrete and particularly in dramatic cantilevers, the structural system he chose again and again for his skyscraper projects after 1936. Built, as has been previously mentioned, at Racine in the form of the Johnson Wax Laboratory Tower in the late 1940s and in the Price Tower at Bartlesville in the 1950s, Wright's most characteristic examples of this type of construction express no support at all; the tower is cut away at its base, just where the eye expects to see a massive junction of tower and earth (figs. 8-15a and 8-16a).

Le Corbusier often expressed a similar structural idea, but in slabs rather than towers. His Maison du Brésil at the Cité Universitaire in Paris is characteristic (fig. 8-15b). Here, the parts of the Maison Dom-Ino are rearranged for an effect of breathtaking balance. The independence of the entry pavilion only reinforces the strength of the structural conception (fig. 8-16b). The treatment of windows, sometimes as infill between masonry elements and sometimes piercing the concrete slabs with a kind of independent force, is similar to Wright's, especially in details such as the setting of glass directly into the masonry and the occasional piercing of glass lights by masonry elements.

The Maison du Brésil, constructed between 1957 and 1959, offers a direct comparison with its earlier neighbor, the Pavillon Suisse of 1930. Similar in planning and structure, the greatest difference between the two buildings is just what marks Le Corbusier's turn toward the Organic school in his later career: the attitudes toward *construction*. The smooth refinement of materials and detailing of the Pavillon Suisse speaks of factory prefabrication (figs. 8-15c and 8-16c). The generalized, abstract surfaces demanded by Le Corbusier in his early years can be

8-15a. Wright: Johnson Wax Laboratory Tower. (Courtesy of Johnson Wax.)

8-15b. Le Corbusier: Maison du Brésil; Cité Universitaire, Paris, 1958–59.

8-15c. Le Corbusier: Pavillon Suisse, Cité Universitaire, Paris, 1930–33.

8-16a. Wright: Johnson Wax Laboratory Tower.

8-16b. Le Corbusier: Maison du Brésil.

8-16c. Le Corbusier: Pavillon Suisse.

achieved only under controlled conditions with sophisticated machinery and organized production. It is with the new plasticity, the rendered surfaces, and the particularity of the Maison du Brésil that Le Corbusier approaches the attitude of Wright toward sophisticated and craftsmanly fieldwork with the assistance of advanced portable machinery. Such typical late elements as his freestanding accordion-pleated stairs were first used by Wright at Fallingwater. His painting and rendering of the concrete surface as well as his stained glass can also be traced back to the Organic school.

Many of these features, as well as patterned window panels, are found in the Maisons Jaoul (fig. 8-17b), mentioned previously as expressing construction in a manner similar to Wright's Robie House. His typical floor pattern in later buildings is an arrangement of rectangular tiles according to harmonic patterns supposed to reflect the proportions of the Modulor. This expression of Organic dogma is an interesting contrast to Wright's treatment of floors, usually red-painted concrete, with a simple joint occurring regularly on the grid. It is a particularly clear example of the exchange between Organic architecture and the International Style in their late work.

At the Lloyd Lewis House of 1939 outside Chicago, Wright expresses the construction system developed from the early Prairie houses through Fallingwater. Approached, the bedroom wing seems to float above the grassy river bank, another comment on the *pilotis* of the International Style. As at Fallingwater, the cantilevered wooden beams are clearly expressed in section, visible from the river itself. The exaggerated pattern of the stepped wood planks is directly analogous to the linear board patterns Le Corbusier molds into his poured concrete (fig. 8-17a). The load-bearing parallel walls of Le Corbusier's

Catalan vault houses tend to produce a highly directional space, often rather dark in inner-layered vaults. This odd configuration is similar to pre-Columbian Mayan vault construction in Mexico, and it is interesting to speculate on the influence of this particular primitive architecture on Le Corbusier, especially since Wright had a highly touted Mayan revival period of his own.

So Wright and Le Corbusier more or less exchanged their earlier positions in the area of technology in a way that advances rather than diverts their previous directions. This is confirmed by the third expressive technical element in Modern architecture, *mechanical systems.* At the Guggenheim Museum, Wright allows the freestanding service tubes, containing ducts, pipes, and an elevator shaft, to intersect his spiral ramps cleanly. A dropped angled soffit above the ramp parapet contains additional mechanical services and the total effect is one of machine precision characteristic of the International Style. Le Corbusier, on the other hand, became interested in the forces of nature and developed elaborate systems for sun protection and for catching rainwater. His roof expression, as has been mentioned, is reminiscent of the Prairie style, and his *brises-soleil,* picked up by Wright in the Price Tower, are often treated in a decorative manner similar to Wright's. This mutual interchange of focus can be summed up in the final of the four elements of the architectural analysis, iconography.

For a look at the *prosaic* level of the iconography of Modernism, four late churches of Wright and three late churches of Le Corbusier will be examined. As a building type, the church, even with its diminished importance in the twentieth century, has probably been the most thoroughly studied in Western architectural history. Cognitively, therefore, its functional and purposive characteristics have been

8-17a. Wright: Lloyd Lewis House, Libertyville, Illinois, 1939.

8-17b. Le Corbusier: Maisons Jaoul, Paris, 1952–56. (Courtesy of Nancy Monroe.)

the best understood. Furthermore, neither Wright nor Le Corbusier were particularly wrapped up in the arcane dogma of the sects they were called upon to house, so that both were able to take a detached and objective approach to the problems at hand. In fact, Wright's churches serve four very different faiths: Methodist, Unitarian, Jewish, and Greek Orthodox. Le Corbusier's are all Roman Catholic, but of different types: pilgrimage, monastic, and parish.

The first Wright church under discussion, the Annie Pfeiffer Chapel of 1938, marks a transition from the early Unity Temple to the later works of the 1940s and 1950s. Both churches have similar cruciform plans based on a square; three sides are galleries on two levels, the fourth being left for the altar, with choir loft above. What is new in the Annie Pfeiffer Chapel is that another centralizing shape, a hexagon, has been superimposed on the square, resulting in a directional space emphasized by the longitudinal skylight on the major axis and, on the outside, thin, winglike slabs stretching along the minor axis. Wright thus resolves the centuries-old conflict between centralized and longitudinal plans in a Modern way, the superimposition of contradictory axes. Entrance to the chapel is nonaxial, achieved through one of four equal corner vestibules marked by cascades of steps.

In the next church, the First Unitarian Church in Madison, Wisconsin, of 1947, Wright again uses a hexagon, marked in the recess under the choir loft; but rather than superimposing a second geometry, he first crosses the church with a Sunday School wing near the entrance and then uses a great gabled roof to draw attention to the altar (fig. 8-18). The roof and cross-shaped plan, of course, are derived from the Prairie style, and it is likely, since Wright was himself Unitarian, that he consciously aimed

for a "housey" rather than a "churchy" building to emphasize the nonmystical nature of that particular religion. From the parking area, the deep entry to the church behind the low eaves is off-center along the Sunday School wing, so that one first senses the longitudinal axis after entering and then is made aware of the vestigial centralizing hexagon.

Probably Wright's finest church, and one of his masterpieces, the Beth Sholom Synagogue was designed in 1954 and built outside of Philadelphia just before his death. There is no clearer manifestation in all his work of a tent built upon a cave. Brilliantly sited at the peak of a hill so that its glazed wigwam top can be seen poking out of the trees from miles away, the synagogue from the outside is an opaque crystalline growth, one of its three equal facades marked for entry by a projecting canopy (fig. 8-19). Immediately upon entering, one is faced with a choice: to descend on axis into the cavelike auditorium below or to turn right or left and climb into the translucent wigwam of the synagogue above. The synagogue floor is gently angled and colored in warm reds and pinks, whereas the wigwam structure is of silver and gray, producing the effect of a cloud settling over a mountain top (fig. 8-20). The altar is on axis, and Wright chose an equilateral triangle for a plan generator, a shape that is intrinsically both axial and centralized. The simultaneous reading of the directed base and the centralized canopy is quite clear and perfect in its balance. In fact, the vertical axis is physically traced by the cable supporting the triangular chandelier that drops through a tiny triangular hole formed by the concrete supporting beams above.

Wright's final church, the Annunciation Orthodox Church in Milwaukee, was designed just before his death and completed in 1961 (fig. 8-21). It has much of the circular detailing of the contemporary

8-18. Wright: First Unitarian Church, Madison, Wisconsin, 1947. (Courtesy of Kathryn A. Smith, Los Angeles.)

Marin County Civic Center. A raised circular seating area is superimposed over a cruciform main floor. It is Wright's most centralized church, not just because of the powerful domed roof, but also because of the subtle off-setting of the altar so that it is not on axis from the entrance. The entrance is marked from the outside by a canopy on one of the four equal facades, similar to the Beth Sholom Synagogue. In the Annie Pfeiffer Chapel, the synagogue, and the Greek Orthodox church, the building is presented as an introverted, self-contained hall into which the visitor steps either directly under a canopy or cir-

8-19. Wright: Beth Sholom Synagogue, Elkins Park, Pennsylvania, 1954.

8-21. Wright: Annunciation Orthodox Church, Milwaukee, 1956. (Courtesy of Kathryn A. Smith, Los Angeles.)

8-20. Wright: Beth Sholom Synagogue.

cumstantially from the side. At the First Unitarian Church, however, the experience of the room of worship is delayed. Strangely, this seems here to support a more casual, less sanctified ambience.

Le Corbusier's Chapelle de Notre-Dame-du-Haut at Ronchamp, designed and built between 1950 and 1955, is one of his most sculptural works, almost more Wrightian than Wright himself in its handcrafted construction and detailing and in its intense relation with its natural surroundings. The axis of the small church is minimized by the strongly asymmetric confrontation between roof and walls, which twist and bend as if in response to terrific natural or supernatural forces (fig. 8-22). There is a sweeping roof that rises to a shaft of light in a manner not dissimilar to Wright's First Unitarian Church, resulting in a play of axes in conflict after the entrance sequence (fig. 8-23). This deemphasizes the eastern orientation in a manner different from the Wrightian super-imposition of a centralizing geometry.

At the monastery of Sainte-Marie-de-la-Tourette, outside of Lyons, the church of 1960 is strongly longitudinal, the axis in fact being inscribed in the floor pavement. Again, however, there is a shaft of light at the corner of the eastern wall that contradicts the central axis (fig. 8-24). Although cross-shaped in plan, the lower transverse arm containing the sacristy and side chapels is dynamically asymmetrical, with the space bursting through and cascading over the chapels below as if dammed by the battered wall of the sacristy across the nave. The longitudinal axis seems to be applied, almost abstracted upon a dynamic and differentiated space. The symmetrical western half of the church, the secular side, is placed in opposition to the strongly asymmetrical eastern end, the spiritual side. The cruciform shape and clerestory lighting of a dim interior relate the church somewhat to Wright's Greek Orthodox church; al-

8-23. Le Corbusier: Chapelle de Notre-Dame-du-Haut.

though the use is quite different—for monks rather than for an urban congregation—the Greek Orthodox ritual requires a screened sanctuary for those parts not to be viewed by the congregation, a peculiarity that is something like the private masses celebrated by the monks in the sunken chapels of La Tourette's cross-arm.

The final church is the Eglise de St. Pierre at Firminy-Vert, designed around 1960 (fig. 8-25). Although it was never constructed, local interest has apparently been maintained and it may yet be realized. This church is, in many respects, a sort of wigwam similar to Wright's Beth Sholom Synagogue. It has cavelike supporting spaces in the base below its lofty, free-form shell and is entered at ground level while the nave itself is a half-level up. The centralized square plan is given axiality by the vertical transition of the walls to a free-form shape approximating a circle shifted against the eastern altar wall. This is the source of light for the church and

8-22. Le Corbusier: Chapelle de Notre-Dame-du-Haut, Ronchamp, 1950. (Courtesy of Nancy Monroe.)

8-24. Le Corbusier: Sainte-Marie-de-la-Tourette. Arbresle, 1960.

should, as in Le Corbusier's other churches, offer the southerly path of the sun as a counterpoint to the geometrically established east-west axis. This regard for natural lighting *as a dynamic force on the building* is an example of Le Corbusier's adoption of Organic principles. The relation to Beth Sholom can also be seen in the canopied entrance on one of the repeated elevations, as well as in the tiered seating.

To turn to the *purposive* aspect of iconographic communication at the prosaic level: how well do these seven churches express their functions? Wright's Annie Pfeiffer Chapel stands more apart from the canopied walks that dominate the rest of Florida Southern College than the other campus buildings do. The church's commanding plastic form with its chime tower proclaims monumentality, and the opacity of its walls, from the outside at least, denote its introverted, sanctified quality. At the same time, the spreading cantilevered roof wings at the sides and the steps leading to the lawn at two of the entrances give the church a distinctive welcoming character appropriate for its function as a campus meeting place. The sky-cave interior focuses daylight on the rostrum and congregation; the light is filtered through a complex skylight system originally designed to hold living flowers. Nature is thus very much a part of the services and the impression of the participant is of congregation rather than of introspection. This impression is reinforced by the tiny dots of sparkling colored glass that pierce the ostensibly solid concrete block walls.

At the First Unitarian Church, Wright establishes the image of the congregational house of worship with his Prairie vocabulary of low spreading roof and asymmetrical, cruciform plan. Within the church, the rostrum is directly in front of the great transparent gable, inviting the assembled to focus on both the one crosses the bridge. Le Corbusier's clear and rational structure is in this way denied by Wright in favor of a more plastic and dramatic cantilever support system. And whereas the supports of the Villa Savoie seem to be placed without regard for the circumstances of its site—such as the approach road—the analogous trellis beams of Fallingwater are not only carefully cut into the surrounding rock but are in one case even bent around a tree.

The presentation by each architect of a precisely defined structural *system* is indicative of a most crucial attitude toward Modern "style" that was common to both of them. In *Vers Une Architecture* Le Corbusier proposes the idea of standardization as the foundation for Modern style.

It is necessary to press on towards the establishment of *standards* in order to face the problem of *perfection*.[20] Here we have the birth of style, that is to say the attainment, universally recognized, of a state of perfection universally felt. . . . The establishment of a standard is developed by organizing rational elements, following a line of direction equally rational. The form and appearance are in no way preconceived, *they are a result*.[21]

Modern architecture, then, is to be formed by the organization of building elements, rationally chosen, into *systems* based on real standards such as function or manufacture. This same idea was espoused by Wright about the same time in his 1927–28 series of articles for *Architectural Record*, "In the Cause of Architecture":

The question is now, how to achieve *style*, how to conserve that quality and profit to the fullest extent by standardization, the soul of the machine, in the work that is "Man."[22] . . . [Style is obtained] first by directly acknowledging the *nature* of the problem presented and

expressing it with a sense of appropriate shape and proportion in terms of the *character* of the materials and the process of work that [is] to make the building.[23]

The clear expression of independent systems of building elements is therefore the key to understanding both the Villa Savoie and Fallingwater as statements of stylistic principles for Modern architecture. In the Villa Savoie, four systems can be detected. The regular grid of structural columns, or *pilotis,* along with the associated beams and framing members, is visible penetrating the second floor behind the openings in the facades. The four facades are almost identical, presenting themselves as a second independent system of screen walls with continuous slots, stretched around the column grid. The third system is the steel-framed windows, which circumstantially fill or bend away from the slots in the facade at each bay, according to the functional requirements of the space behind. The fourth system is the rising service core, visible from the outside as the curved stair that penetrates from the ground through both second floor and roof to become a freestanding element above. Each of these systems has a quality of independence from the others. Although the house is full of incidental distortions and adjustments at points of intersection between the systems, none seems to determine the other three. There is a sense of coordinated order rather than the hierarchical order characteristic of architecture of the past.

The same sort of expression occurs at Fallingwater. Three systems are immediately visible. The horizontally spreading trays seem to be laid out independently of the supporting stone core system. The red-painted steel mullions of the ribbon window system bend around between the trays, sometimes

2-1a. Wright: Kaufmann House, Bear Run, Pennsylvania, 1935.

2-1b. Le Corbusier: Villa Savoie, Poissy, 1928.

2-2a. Wright: Kaufmann House.

2-2b. Le Corbusier: Villa Savoie.

along the edges and sometimes not. Where they touch the stone core, the glass is fitted directly into the masonry without terminating mullions. There is here as at the Villa Savoie a quality of indeterminacy in the relation of the carefully defined systems, each reflecting its own particularities of function and fabrication.

These two famous houses stand, then, as extremely important historical statements about the nature of a relevant Modern architecture. Correspondences between the two have the nature of a dialogue in stone, glass, and metal. One of the most famous and important of such statements is made at the entry to the Villa Savoie where a standard lavatory is presented as an overt symbol of the mass-produced functional object (figs. 2-3a,b). At the entry to Fallingwater, a natural spring spills into a pool made from rocks, denying the factory-made object with an element particular to the function and nature of the site. There is an emphasis on diagonal upward movement at the Villa Savoie, made through carefully detailed parapets and railings around the main stair and ramp (figs. 2-4a,b). Horizontal extension is celebrated at Fallingwater with suspended stairs that drop from the cantilevered trays.

From within the Villa Savoie, every view to the surrounding countryside is framed, even to the extent of freestanding exterior screens at the second floor and roof terraces (figs. 2-5a,b). There is a resulting feeling of privacy and enclosure, a separation from nature. But at Fallingwater, Wright consciously denies the framing of the windows, first by making the mullions as thin as possible and most strikingly at the corners where the verticals disappear altogether and the glass is mitered. This is a denial of enclosure, an emphasized extension to the surrounding woods and an insistence on a connection between man and nature. At the Villa Savoie, the small detached

2-3a. Wright: Kaufmann House.　　　　　　2-3b. Le Corbusier: Villa Savoie.

2-4a. Wright: Kaufmann House.   2-4b. Le Corbusier: Villa Savoie.

2-5a. Wright: Kaufmann House.

2-5b. Le Corbusier: Villa Savoie.

2-6a. Wright: Kaufmann House.   2-6b. Le Corbusier: Villa Savoie.

fireplace stands alone, a manufactured object in the intense flow of open space achieved through the minimizing of separation between rooms. At Fallingwater, the fireplace is built into an enormous rock left as found on the site, around which the open space seems to swirl.

The dialogue between Le Corbusier and Wright, then, is in accord about the expression of standardized systems, the importance of clearly revealed function and structure, and the excitement of dynamically charged open planning (figs. 2-6a, b and 2-7a, b). There is, however, disagreement about the relation of man and nature and about the exact use of the machine in fabrication. The Villa Savoie is introspective, sitting detached and remote above its grassy site. Fallingwater stretches itself out in every direction, reaching for a union between the man-made and the natural. The Villa Savoie celebrates the perfection of machine-finished surfaces and the purity of standardized objects. Fallingwater relates custom-fabricated objects to machine-finished surfaces both smooth and rough, contrasting the homogeneity of steel, glass, and painted plaster with the natural surfaces of stone, water, and foliage. The resulting dialogue is sensual as well as intellectual and can be thoroughly appreciated only through direct experience.

The correspondences between the Villa Savoie and Fallingwater support the contention that Wright had Le Corbusier's masterpiece in mind when he sat down to design this house for Edgar Kaufmann, Sr., in 1935, three years after the exhibition at the Museum of Modern Art. He appears to have laid out the design in a single night, which suggests that he had already thought through specific responses to what he perceived to be the tenets of the International Style as epitomized by the Villa Savoie. This would also account for the abrupt break with

2-7a. Wright: Kaufmann House.

2-7b. Le Corbusier: Villa Savoie.

earlier work that Fallingwater represents for him, a discontinuity singular in his career of rigorous development toward clearly defined goals.

Even more important for the development of Modern style are the works that begin his late career: those that he created between 1936 and 1940. In these seminal buildings—the Johnson Wax Headquarters, Florida Southern College, and the first Usonian houses—Wright distills the essentials of the International Style and strikes out in a direction determined by a new conception of structure and materials. Although his later career will be studied in depth later, it is important here to emphasize these initial buildings as his response to the International Style.

The articulated post-and-beam structure associated with the International Style—and so apparent in the Villa Savoie—was anathema to Wright. He saw it as the most *rétardataire* of holdovers from the Classical past and set out in the late thirties on a series of dramatic demonstrations of cantilever construction in response. The floating balconies of Fallingwater have already been mentioned, but reference should be made as well to the semicircular canopy, suspended only on the thinnest of steel rods, that steps up the hillside behind the main house. Another experiment along these lines at the Johnson Wax Headquarters of 1936 was integrated with the deepest meaning of the building itself, the symbolic analogy with nature.

Consistent in Wright's architecture is the organization of building elements into three or four mutually independent systems that he expressed as analogues of natural elements interpreted as they relate to human function. At Fallingwater, the rough-dressed stone quarried at the site represents the ground itself, from which, in Wright's view, all else grows into the light.[24] There is a graded develop-ment—an increase of abstraction and of the degree of finishing of materials—from the rocks left visible around and beneath the house to the boulder around which the hearth is built, then to the dressed stones of the supporting masses and floor surface, and finally to the painted and smooth-finished trays of the balconies. This striation motif, carried explicitly from the materials found on the site into the construction of the house itself, is enriched by the steel-and-glass window system that runs between the parapets like the stream below, flowing between the rock embankments. The three elements of nature—rocks, water, and light—that Wright distinguished at the site, each reacting with but independent of the others, were translated into the component systems of the house. It is to this perception of the coordinated systems of nature as analogous to the construction of buildings that Wright's term *Organic architecture* seems to refer.

At the Johnson Wax Headquarters, the site was a nondescript block in a semiindustrial urban area of Racine, Wisconsin. The component systems here, therefore, are not made from direct analogies with the nature of the site but from three of the most advanced of mass-produced construction techniques: brick, glass, and reinforced concrete. The meaning of Johnson Wax appears in horizontal strata, beginning at the base (fig. 2-8). If approached from the main street, only two systems are visible: a massive wall of brick broken by thin ribbons of glass tubes. At ground level, the brick dominates: It follows the outline of the building in a simple rectangle determined by the nature of the brick as a building unit. The first layer of glass appears as a minor break in the wall, except at the corner where the mitered glass tubes suddenly bubble over, bending the wall above into a curve. The transcendence of glass over the brick is completed at the cornice

2-8. Wright: Johnson Wax Headquarters, Racine, 1936. (Courtesy of Johnson Wax.)

2-9. Wright: Johnson Wax Headquarters.

where a wider band of glass blisters out and over the top, causing a break in the thin line of the brick parapet just where it curves at the corner. Thus the massive, solid appearance of the brick wall at its base is changed by the action of the glass to that of a thin screen at the top.

At the entry from either side street, the third system becomes visible (fig. 2-9). Thin, tapered concrete columns with broad circular crowns strain against the apparent weight of the massive brick walls they carry. But in the procession beneath the entry loggia, through the glass doors into the lobby and finally into the main hall itself, the columns thrust higher and higher until the brick mass is reduced to the lightest of bridges floating between the entry foyer and the workroom, the columns rising beyond to the skylit ceiling of glass to reveal the fragile, screenlike quality of the brick walls, totally reversing the impression first received from the exterior (fig. 2-10).

These columns with their cantilevered crowns represent a post-supported structural system exactly the opposite of that proposed by Le Corbusier in the Dom-Ino system. There, columns at the corners of a square bay provided foursquare support. But Wright saw this as an oversimplification of structural analysis. In any reinforced-concrete structure, the columns would be tied into the slab with steel bars, forming a rigid and continuous joint between columns and slab. Thus, the area supported by any one column can be seen as a module formed by the centerlines of the bays *between* the columns. This reversal of the module, so clearly articulated by Wright in his circular column capitals separated by glass tubes, is analogous to the departure of English Gothic fan vaulting in the thirteenth and fourteenth centuries from the French high Gothic structural system of the twelfth century.

Johnson Wax, then, can be read as a dramatic

interaction between three independent systems. The brick earth element is gradually conquered by the growth of circular concrete plant- or life-element columns that reach toward the glass tubes of the sky element. The detailing of these tubes derives from a sophisticated perception of the possibilities of factory-produced curves and machine-assisted field joints: They sweep around in broad circles, producing bubbly profiles where they are mitered at the corners.

When the laboratory tower was added to the Johnson complex after World War II, the basic earth/sky reading of the administration building was enriched. From the parking lot approach, the layout reads like a traditional Japanese Buddhist temple plan, with a gatehouse, pagoda, and hall in sequence on axis. The central core supporting the tower confirms the analogy. The tower rises from behind a low brick wall, but through the main gate a deep space seems to penetrate continuously beyond the tower (fig. 2-11). The structure of the tower is revealed from the gate itself to be a narrow central core with the floors cantilevered from it (fig. 2-12). Behind the glass tubing of the double-height floors, circular mezzanines are visible. Again, the growth of a circular supporting element lifts brick to the sky.

The Johnson Wax complex is a commentary on the machine esthetic of the International Style. Just as Le Corbusier used standard glass laboratory beakers as vases in the Pavillon de l'Ésprit Nouveau, Wright chose Pyrex laboratory tubing for all the glass in the building. It is fitted into special metal frames and wired into place. This adaptation of a standardized material is an important element of distinction between Wright's and Le Corbusier's work. Wright maintains a stronger element of custom fabrication in his detailing. He celebrates particular applications of standardized products, whereas Le

2-10. Wright: Johnson Wax Headquarters.

2-11. Wright: Johnson Wax Laboratory Tower, Racine, 1944. 2-12. Wright: Johnson Wax Laboratory Tower.

Corbusier stresses the independence of factory-made building systems.

This distinction between the two is maintained even into their late works, at the time of the closest connection between their styles. Consider in comparison the construction and detailing of the walkway piers at Wright's campus at Florida Southern College in Lakeland, Florida (1938) and the main supporting piers of Le Corbusier's Unité d'Habitation at Marseilles (1947) (figs. 2-13a, b). Wright's piers have a complex, angular shape (fig. 2-14). To form the poured concrete, composite wooden formwork was used in such a way that it could be dismantled when the concrete had set and reused for the next pier. A distinctive pattern is imposed upon sections of the surface. The pattern is made by nailing pieces of wood inside the form; its angular nature makes it easy to cut the pieces and assemble them. Le Corbusier's piers are similarly complex in their swelling curve, but the detailing of the formwork expresses the standardized boards making up the form. They are used directly with minimal adaptation to the particular project, the two halves being separated by a simple reveal. Futhermore, the Marseilles piers are left unfinished in acknowledgment of the method of construction, whereas Wright's piers are finished smooth and painted off-white. Le Corbusier accepts the independence of standardized construction methods as an esthetic opportunity; Wright stresses the craftsmanly adaptation of construction techniques to the design standards of a particular project. Le Corbusier celebrates mass production in the factory; Wright celebrates the skill of the craftsman in using portable machine tools in the field.

The Florida Southern College campus itself is another important achievement at the beginning of Wright's late career. The master plan dates from 1938 and was executed with certain changes and

2-13a. Wright: piers, Florida Southern College, Lakeland, 1938.

2-13b. Le Corbusier: piers, Unité d'Habitation, Marseilles, 1947.

2-14. Wright: Florida Southern College.

only in part over the next twenty years. A total of seven buildings designed by Wright were finally incorporated, each of them different. The college is the only built example of Wright's planning ideas and offers a unique experience of his design.

The campus employs a Jeffersonian *parti*. Thomas Jefferson's University of Virginia campus is based on a *theme* and a *center*. The theme is the series of Classical colonnades that shelters the walkways surrounding the central quadrangle. The center is the Rotunda, which houses the library. At Florida Southern, the theme again is a series of walkways and the center is the Annie Pfeiffer Chapel, a large auditorium standing free from the walkways near the crest of the hill. Just as Jefferson provided a variety of Classical treatments for the ten minor buildings along the colonnades at Virginia, so Wright designed minor buildings that derive in different ways from the modular pier system supporting the walkway canopy. But Virginia's straightforward rectangular plan is transformed at Florida into a more open arrangement based on sixty- as well as ninety-degree angles. This overt contradiction of a rectilinear grid is confirmed by several instances where the joints in the concrete paving are aligned with the main Pfeiffer Chapel axis, even when they occur in a walkway at sixty degrees to the axis. At one point, this detail is carried through a flight of steps (fig. 2-15). Such a costly insistence on the denial of the grid in the face of severe financial restrictions—the campus was built mostly by students on work/study funds—can be interpreted as another comment on the International Style Cartesian grid. There is also at Florida Southern College another variation on post-and-beam structure. Here the walkway piers are made so massive that the paper-thin canopy they support seems almost inconsequential in context. The canopy seems to hover above the strip of sidewalk, the piers marching alongside like sentinels.

The theme of the piers is varied at the approaches to the different buildings along the walkways. At the library, they cluster in groups (fig. 2-16). At the administration building, they are paired to form an esplanade detailed with lacy trellises (fig. 2-17). At the domestic arts building, they form a tunnel (fig. 2-18). At the science building, the canopy breaks into a sequence of floating planes (fig. 2-19). This study of the structural and architectural variations on a particular support system can be seen as the equivalent to the experimentation with Classical orders at Virginia, but Wright directs attention not to the historical values of a civilization past but rather to the structural and esthetic possibilities for the future.

At Florida Southern College the thin, stretched white planes so evocative of the International Style are opposed, as at Fallingwater, to a more typically

2-15. Wright: Florida Southern College.

2-16. Wright: Florida Southern College.

2-18. Wright: Florida Southern College.

2-17. Wright: Florida Southern College.

2-19. Wright: Florida Southern College.

Wrightian system, in this case pierced concrete block. The smooth winged mass of the Pfeiffer Chapel is made to lift above its block base (fig. 2-20). Inside, the stained glass particles in the blocks sparkle in the shadows as the white mass above soars upward into the light through a complex series of skylights (fig. 2-21). The four supporting piers are almost invisible in the shadows, enhancing the image of floating masses.

In numbers of progeny, the most significant of Wright's responses to the International Style was the Usonian house. The catalog of the Museum of Modern Art exhibition on Modern architecture of 1932 had made it clear that the primary building task of the twentieth century was to provide adequate housing for all.[25] The reply that Wright was making with his Usonian house was very different from the International Style idea of mass-produced houses from factories. Instead, the Usonian used relatively cheap, lightweight materials in standard sizes and configurations that could be easily hand-fitted into the house at the site with the help of portable tools and a small table saw. The houses were so easy to build (many clients built their own) and so energy conscious that they are still far ahead of contemporary American building practice forty years later. Along with Le Corbusier's classic series of studio-houses of the 1920s, the Usonian houses represent the most profound and important declaration of a Modern style based on the coordinated integration of independent building systems into a composite whole.

The Loren Pope House, built in Virginia in 1939–40 (and since moved to a site near Washington, D.C.), is an example of a typical Usonian house (fig. 2-22). The component systems expressed in the house are the brick base and service core, the wood and glass of the walls, and the deeply cantilevered roof and clerestory. Although sharply dif-

2-20. Wright: Annie Pfeiffer Chapel, Florida Southern College, Lakeland, 1938.

ferentiated from each other and starkly detailed in the interest of economy, the systems become enriched by the subtle interactions among them. The interruption of the boards of the wall at the service side of the approach by the brick core is turned back on itself with the reacting interruption of the wall system by a standard wood-framed window (fig. 2-23). The jigsawed lights of the clerestory are carried down into the walls at the ends of the two main wings (fig. 2-24). It is through such incidents beyond mere detailing that quite simple building systems are enriched in meaning. The relationship of this to function and circulation, to the environmental circumstances of the site, and to a larger view of living in American society will be explored in greater depth further on.

What has been shown through this analysis of some of Wright's work of the late 1930s is the

2-21. Wright: Annie Pfeiffer Chapel.

2-22. Wright: Loren Pope House, Virginia, 1939–40.

2-23. Wright: Loren Pope House.

2-24. Wright: Loren Pope House.

degree to which his work was related to the International Style. The basic similarities are finally more significant than superficial or circumstantial differences of construction technique or site characteristics. These similarities stem from an attitude held in common by both Wright and Le Corbusier that a truly Modern style would depend on an esthetic recognition of standardization of building components, a recognition made manifest in the way each of them coordinates systems of components in his buildings.

Wright confirmed his mastery of International Style principles in two exhibitions at the Museum of Modern Art in the late 1930s. One, in 1938, was a small selection of drawings and photographs of Fallingwater, his answer to the Villa Savoie. The other, in 1940, was a comprehensive exhibition of his work to date, and he actively solicited none other than Henry-Russell Hitchcock—who had, as has been shown, virtually dismissed him as an active contributor to Modern architecture in the 1932 exhibition catalog—to write a critical study of his work, entitled *In the Nature of Materials,* an explicit statement by Wright of one of the most important distinctions between his work and the International Style. So, although his seventy years' production has its own inner coherence, no critical evaluation of it can claim to be comprehensive without taking account of the significant influence on his work of the International Style in the 1930s.

By the same token, the profound change in Le Corbusier's own style during the same period can be interpreted as his confrontation with elements of Organic architectural theory. Although any direct influence by Wright would seem impossible to prove, certain events in Le Corbusier's career between the late 1920s and World War II seem to have made him aware of the possibility for a larger, more comprehensive modern architecture than he had been

practicing. The 1932 exhibition marked the high point of Le Corbusier's fame and acceptance, but it should not be forgotten that much of his work, particularly in large-scale planning, was not to be built and remained singularly theoretical. As a result of his fame, he was able to incite interest in these theoretical projects, but after Pessac none was built until the post–World War II Unités d'Habitation. The beginning of this period of retrenchment and reevaluation was touched off by the failure of his submissions to the League of Nations Headquarters competitions in 1927 and 1929. In a series of highly publicized confrontations, the conservative architectural and political establishments joined forces to defeat the proposals of radical Modernists generally and Le Corbusier in particular. It was a pattern that would continue throughout the 1930s in a number of competitions, projects, and plans that Le Corbusier would never see realized. He was forced to sharpen the distinction of the new architecture he was trying to establish from the still-living Neoclassical tradition representing, as he said himself, "la Patrie, et la Nation, et la Beauté, et l'Art et tout ce qu'on voudra."[26] Particularly difficult for him to accept at this time was the application by other architects of International Style forms, materials, and methods upon essentially Neoclassical plans, particularly in America. The connections with Greek and Renaissance architecture and with Platonic forms that Le Corbusier had suggested for Modern architecture in *Vers Une Architecture* in 1922 had become problematic and it was necessary to find a more contemporary justification for his style.

The experience of practice, the studies of growth patterns of towns that he undertook for city plans (most notably from airplanes and zeppelins), and the unfortunate weathering qualities of some of his early buildings had all influenced him to increase the empirical element in his research. His development of the *brise-soleil* during the 1930s as a result of solar heat gain in the Cité du Réfuge and Pavillon Suisse in Paris and his construction of several country houses using rough, local materials are manifestations of this new tendency. The advance in his style can be detected even between the Purist statement of geometric shapes at the entry to the Cité du Réfuge and the more plastic and organic entry at the Pavillon Suisse. The culmination of this change would be the development of the Modulor, a system of proportion based on the Fibonacci series, a mathematical progression found in many natural processes such as the harmonics of sound waves and the growth of plants. The Modulor was to be embodied in the first constructed work of his later style, the Unité d'Habitation in Marseilles of 1947.

In an issue of *Zodiac* that appeared in the fall of 1959, Le Corbusier published the following statement commemorating Wright, who had died earlier that year:

Frank Lloyd Wright fut certainement un grand personnage très considéré.

Ce que je connais pertinement de lui c'est qu'il a été bafoué pendant presque toute sa vie et que, subitement, les trompettes de la gloire ont éclaté dans le ciel américain et mondial. Et ceci lui était bien dû.

Personnellement, je n'ai pas connu Wright. Dans un banquet, offert à lui et à Auguste Perret, par le Directeur Général des Beaux-Arts à Paris, durant l'Exposition de 1937, assis à un bout de table, je me suis levé au dessert et je me suis permis de dire: «M. le Directeur Général, Messieurs, je salue ici les deux étoiles du firmament architectural contemporain.»

Auguste Perret était assis très à gauche du Directeur Général des Beaux-Arts et Wright très à droite, environ six mètres de distance l'un de l'autre. Votre serviteur était à une extrêmité du fer à cheval formé par les tables.

Chacun de nous est une unité authentique souriante ou à rebrousse-poil, combattus à cause de l'«idée,» combattant l'«idée,» son «idée» combattue par les autres. C'est un cercle fatal mais qui n'apporte nul désespoir philosophique. Ceux qui ont des idées sont en général des gens coriaces.

Wright laisse un immense souvenir et il laisse son oeuvre.[27]

Frank Lloyd Wright undoubtedly was a great and highly respected figure.

What I know for a fact about him is that he was scoffed at almost all his life and that, suddenly, the trumpets of glory sounded for him in America and around the world. And this was only his due.

I never knew Wright personally. At a banquet given for him and Auguste Perret by the Director General of the Beaux-Arts in Paris during the Exposition of 1937, I rose from my seat at the end of the table during dessert and permitted myself to say: "Director General, gentlemen, I salute here the two stars in the firmament of contemporary architecture."

Auguste Perret was seated at the left of the Director General and Wright at his right, about six meters from each other. Your servant was at one end of a horseshoe formed by the tables. Each of us is a true individual, smiling or prickly, embattled in the cause of the Ideal, fighting the Ideal itself, his Ideal attacked by the others. It is a fatal circle, but it brings no philosophical despair. Those who have Ideals tend to be thick-skinned in general.

Wright leaves a tremendous legacy and he leaves his work.

Le Corbusier's statement is similar in tone to Wright's 1927 review of *Vers Une Architecture* (see chapter 1) in its wary acknowledgement of Wright's greatness and its distinctively regretful combativeness. The most likely inference is that Le Corbusier, like Wright, was well aware of his rival's oeuvre, of its importance and of its consequence for his own work.

Most striking is Le Corbusier's reference to the 1937 banquet at which Wright had been honored.

In many ways, the circumstances of the 1932 Museum of Modern Art exhibition were now reversed. Here was Wright resurgent, amazing the architectural world with his brand-new Kaufmann House and Johnson Wax Headquarters and making a claim to international renown. And here was Le Corbusier, professionally bogged down in a series of city plans, particularly for Algiers, that would most likely never be realized, as he must have begun to see in 1937. Olgivanna Wright remembered the occasion thus:

We were invited to a dinner given by the architects in honor of Mr. Wright. I sat between two French architects: August Perret and de Huysman. . . .
[Later on, to Mr. Wright] I quoted M. Perret as saying, "The contemporary French architect, le Corbusier, and all that he represents passes. It is only a phase, because a nation which negates its past has no future and I believe that France has a future.[28]

It is not likely that the scorn of his former mentor Perret was unknown to Le Corbusier. For him, the occasion of the banquet must have been a blow to his pride at a moment when, like Wright five years earlier, he was at his most vulnerable. This would explain why he chose to reflect on it in his memorial of 1959. Perhaps he even had had some inkling of what the Kaufmann house would represent, some deep awareness of dialogue with Wright at the professional if not the personal level.

It will be shown further on that the two major distinctions between Le Corbusier and Wright were their attitudes toward factory production and their ideas about the relation of man and nature. It is in this crucial period for both architects, the 1930s, that each considers the view of the other on modern systems of production and, to a lesser extent, on the importance of natural form and the geometry of growth. The man/nature issue was more or less set aside by Wright's focusing on the suburb and Le Corbusier's on the city as the appropriate habitat for modern man. For although there is no great difference between the way the Maisons Jaoul and the Robie House occupy their sites or, on the other hand, between Wright's Mile-High Illinois tower proposal and Le Corbusier's park of Unités, suggested for various locations, each architect created most convincingly in his favored milieu and it may some day be shown that even this difference was more polemic than real. But, certainly, important similarities exist between the work of the two, a circumstance that can be illuminated by a comparative look at their professional careers and backgrounds.

3 Wright and Le Corbusier as Kin:
Careers in Comparison

With the exception of the 1932 Museum of Modern Art exhibition, there appears to have been no direct influence of the work of either Wright or Le Corbusier on the other. However, it is too easy to conclude from this that their thinking was unrelated. The kinship between the two is the historical fact that each was the guiding force behind a revolution in architectural thought. From this it follows that either *two* discrete architectural revolutions brought about two kinds of architecture in this century or else that both men were involved at some deep level in the same movement. The former interpretation is finally untenable, although valiant efforts have been made to carry it through, most notably by Sigfried Giedion in *Space, Time and Architecture*.[29] The latter argument, therefore, is closer to the truth and many historians have attempted to develop it, usually stumbling over Wright's career after 1910. Conventionally, it has been assumed that Wright's influence on Modern architecture ended with his Prairie period and that the remainder of his career is no more than an interesting side show to the main event of the International Style. But it is necessary to go much further than this in acknowledging the strong and vital connection between Wright and Le Corbusier; an account must be made of the influence of historical forces brought to bear on both men by the developing civilization of which they were part, forces that were surprisingly similar, as will be demonstrated by the following comparison of their careers.

Background

Both Frank Lloyd Wright and Le Corbusier (known, of course, by his given name of Charles-Edouard Jeanneret before 1920) lived in provincial towns during their childhoods. Music was important in both their families and each of them had a strong-willed mother who had a say in her son's choice of career. Wright was particularly influenced by his years of working on the farm of his mother's family in Wisconsin, years that would yield a lasting love of nature and a feeling for the particularities of site and environment. Le Corbusier, on the other hand, seems to have been most affected by his time spent studying at the local art school in La Chaux-de-Fonds in Switzerland where his family lived. He learned to be a watchmaker and developed an interest in the

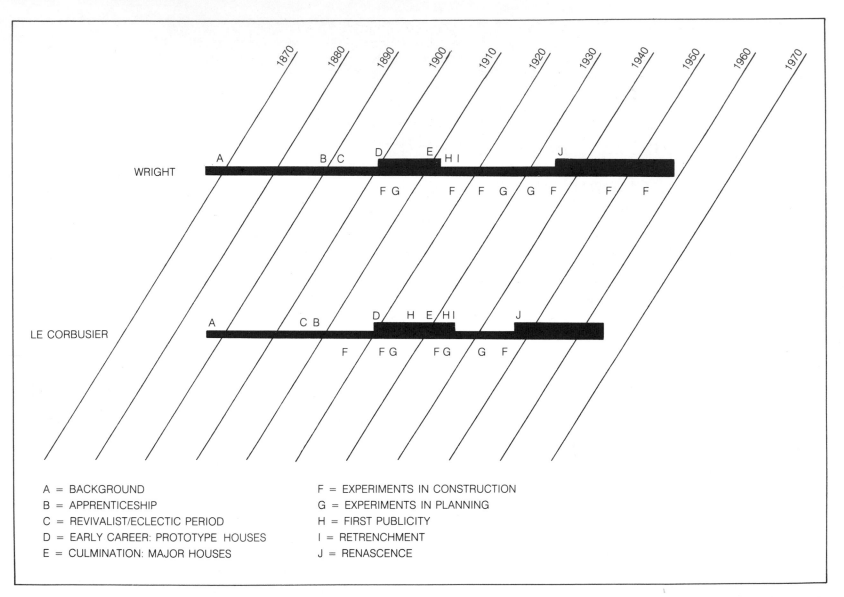

WRIGHT

LE CORBUSIER

1870 1880 1890 1900 1910 1920 1930 1940 1950 1960 1970

A = BACKGROUND
B = APPRENTICESHIP
C = REVIVALIST/ECLECTIC PERIOD
D = EARLY CAREER: PROTOTYPE HOUSES
E = CULMINATION: MAJOR HOUSES

F = EXPERIMENTS IN CONSTRUCTION
G = EXPERIMENTS IN PLANNING
H = FIRST PUBLICITY
I = RETRENCHMENT
J = RENASCENCE

3-1.

fabrication and assembly of parts for manufactured objects. A local teacher, one Charles L'Éplattenier, was particularly influential in showing him the connection between esthetics and the rational design of parts for manufacture.

Apprenticeship

Each architect-to-be spent his apprenticeship in the office of a designer famous for his contribution to the development of a modern structural system. Wright worked with Louis Sullivan, one of the leaders of the steel-framed skyscraper architects of the Chicago School. Although Wright's work was soon to become independent of Sullivan's direct influence, he acknowledged throughout his life the support that Sullivan had given him at this crucial period in his career. Le Corbusier worked with Auguste Perret, an innovator in the development of reinforced-concrete design. And just as Wright produced his first independent masterpiece, the Winslow House in River Forest, Illinois, of 1893, with resources he gathered from his time with Sullivan, Le Corbusier's Dom-Ino system for the construction of housing goes back to ideas under development in Perret's studio when he worked there.

Revivalist/Eclectic Period

Both Wright and Le Corbusier pursued eclecticism during their early careers. Wright used colonial Palladian (Blossom House, Chicago, 1892), Dutch colonial (MacArthur House, Chicago, 1892), Tudor (Moore House, Oak Park, 1895), and especially Italian Renaissance (Charnley House, Chicago, 1891; and Winslow House). Le Corbusier produced houses in the chalet style popular around La Chaux-de-Fonds.

Most startling in comparison with Wright's early work is his Villa Jeanneret-Perret, done for his family in 1912. The broad, tiled hip roof floating above a massive block defined by a ledge at the sill of the second-story windows is quite similar to that of the Winslow House, as is the centrality of the facades, the framing of the central features, and the penetration of the main blocks by semicylindrical bays (figs. 3-2a,b). Le Corbusier's finest house of this period, the Villa Schwob of 1916, is less overtly comparable to Wright's masterpiece, but the symmetry and definition of mass are again similar. Wright's decision to emphasize the roof as a clear and independent element in the design of his future houses can be seen in the Winslow House, as can Le Corbusier's strict denial, through the use of a heavy abstracted cornice, of anything but a flat roof, invisible from the ground, at the Villa Schwob.

Each man also made an important step toward independence at this point in his career. Wright refused an offer to attend the École des Beaux-Arts in Paris, to be paid for by one of his clients. Le Corbusier, meeting his former employer Perret on a trip to Constantinople, decided not to accept the latter's offer of a job working on the important commission for the Théâtre des Champs Élysées. Both men chose an independent path, a conscious refusal of the established route to big-time success.

Early Career: Prototype Houses

Wright's persistence in struggling toward the Prairie style is evident along the streets of Oak Park, River Forest, Hyde Park, and the other suburbs of Chicago, where his earliest houses are located. Ornamental friezes are tried (Winslow House; and Heller House, Hyde Park, 1896). The roofs, already geometrized,

3-2a. Wright: Winslow House, River Forest, Illinois, 1893.

3-2b. Le Corbusier: Villa Jeanneret-Perret, La Chaux-de-Fonds, 1912. (Courtesy of Fondation Le Corbusier.)

are placed high (Fricke-Martin House, Oak Park, 1901; and W. E. Martin House, Oak Park, 1902) and low (Williams House, River Forest, 1895). Windows organized into horizontal bands appear (Heller House; and Rollin Furbeck House, Oak Park, 1897). Finally, the Prairie house is born in the Bradley and Willits Houses (Kankakee, 1900, and Highland Park, 1901, respectively). The Bradley House is important for understanding Wright's insistent denial of Japanese influence on his wood-and-stucco houses. The wooden detailing of the Bradley House is heavy and large-scale, but clean; it represents a transition between Wright's eclectic Tudor houses—not dissimilar to Le Corbusier's chalets—and the delicately scaled Prairie houses of 1900–1910.

Le Corbusier's development was more sporadic in terms of completed buildings, due to the interruption of World War I. But his involvement during the war in running a small brick factory, designing a few industrial buildings, and developing prototypes for mass housing shows clearly the direction of his thought. Although Wright's influence had been felt throughout Europe by his time, there is no certain indication that Le Corbusier took any interest in it. He felt he had developed his architecture entirely on his own and was usually prickly about acknowledging immediate influence. His low-cost housing prototype, the Maison Citrohan of 1920, was based on the technology of mass production and developed its esthetic, through the Dom-Ino system, from that. His attitude toward function was general and minimalist: He had come to admire the simplicity of monastic life on a visit to the monastery at Ema. There is a matter-of-fact directness about his attitude toward construction that manifests itself in the clean detailing and simplified joints characteristic of his houses of this period.

Culmination: Major Houses

Since both architects' early production of buildings other than residences was relatively sparse, it is through their houses that the development of their esthetic can be seen most clearly. Wright's culminating masterpieces are usually considered to be the Robie (1906) and Coonley (1907) Houses, although in a sense these represent the end of a road for him. Lavish in detail, sophisticated in massing, the only important building that carries this particular attitude any further is the Imperial Hotel in Tokyo of 1915, properly seen as overly rich and *rétardataire* for its date. In considering the implications of his early architecture for the future, it is important to stress the significance of the Hardy House (Racine, 1905), the second Mrs. Thomas Gale House (Oak Park, 1904?), and the series of late Prairie houses based on the Isabel Roberts House (River Forest, 1908). These have a directness and an abstract quality that are astounding, considering when they were built.

For Le Corbusier, the Villa Stein at Garches and Villa Savoie at Poissy, 1927 and 1929, respectively, represent final statements of solutions for suburban plots (like the Robie House) and country estates (like the Coonley House). The Villa Savoie would be developed into such culminating masterpieces of his late career as the Villa Shodhan and Governor's Palace in India of the 1950s. But there was another prototype, appearing in project form in 1920 as the Maisons Monol, which consisted of low, parallel vaulted shells of massive construction based on vernacular Mediterranean village sources. One was built, the Maison Week-end outside Paris in 1935, and would be developed into the Villa Sarabhai, contemporary with the Villa Shodhan and also in India.

In their public buildings, both architects made

highly original statements that provided *motives* for the future. Wright's Larkin building in Buffalo of 1903 anticipates the Johnson Wax Headquarters thirty years later in its *parti* of mezzanines surrounding a central skylit work area and its massive exterior walls. His Unity Temple in Oak Park of 1904 would be developed through the Annie Pfeiffer Chapel and through Beth Sholom Synagogue of 1954 in Philadelphia. Le Corbusier's hostel for the Salvation Army in Paris and Pavillon Suisse at the Cité Universitaire were the first manifestations of his Cartesian skyscraper, the most important new building type of the twentieth century. Both buildings point directly through his plans of the 1930s to the Únite block at Marseilles.

Early Experiments with Construction Systems

Wright and Le Corbusier both understood the importance that industrial processes and new materials would have for construction in the twentieth century. Although going no further at first than simplifying the detailing and ornament of his houses, Wright eventually gave consideration to new methods of building in brick, wood, or concrete in the mass housing scheme he proposed for Edward Waller in the early 1900s. He also examined steel-framed prefabricated systems and actually got a few wood-and-stucco Redi-Cut houses built. His involvement in reinforced concrete was typically thorough, and the brick-veneered Larkin Building and aggregate-faced Unity Temple were many years ahead of their time.

Le Corbusier, of course, developed reinforced concrete for use in mass-produced houses, although only prototypes were realized. At Pessac, however, he explored the use of sprayed concrete (Gunite), and although the process had to be discontinued there, he later used it again at Ronchamp, as Wright did at the Guggenheim Museum. Le Corbusier worked with the Voisin automobile and aircraft manufacturers to develop a prefabricated system, the Maisons Monol, which used asbestos sandwich panels. His interest in glass-and-steel began with the construction of Pierre Chareau's Maison de Verre in Paris around 1930. Le Corbusier adopted this construction in his small apartment building at the Porte Molitor of 1933.

Early Experiments in Planning

Wright's interest in large-scale planning was limited to the suburbs, where he developed systems of Prairie houses placed on typical suburban blocks, and to the country, in such projects as the Como Orchard summer colony. His apparent rejection of city planning as such may stem from a resentment of the then fashionable "City Beautiful" movement led by Daniel Burnham, a planning approach, centered in Chicago, that had grown out of the 1892 Columbian Exposition in that city. Since Wright felt that the Exposition had virtually ended Louis Sullivan's influence on American architecture, he may in his own first flush of fame have irrevocably chosen a direction that would make impossible for him any serious involvement in the growing American interest in city planning. At any rate, it was not until the 1920s that he again became interested in planning relatively independent and large-scale projects, first with the San-Marcos-in-the-Desert project and later with Broadacre City.

Le Corbusier, however, was obsessed with the idea of city planning, most likely stemming from his supposed familiarity with Tony Garnier's plans for

Lyons around 1915. The destruction of whole towns in eastern France during World War I must have made the opportunity for large-scale planning more real to him than it ever was to Wright. Several times during the 1920s, Le Corbusier was able to participate in exhibitions that not only provided a platform for him to air his views on La Ville Contemporaine, La Ville Radieuse, and Le Plan Voisin, but even allowed him to construct—most importantly at Stuttgart in 1927—his own pavilion, demonstrating at full scale his construction and planning principles. All this is, of course, in starkest contrast to the experiences of Wright, who, having been made suspicious of exhibitions by Sullivan's experience of 1892, had his attitude confirmed by the notorious failure of the committee of architects planning Chicago's Century of Progress Exhibition of 1933 to invite even his opinions, let alone his participation.

First Influence: Publicity

Both architects were masters at public relations. Far from being ignored by the press, Wright's early career was closely followed by the architectural publications of his time, especially *Architectural Record*, which published major articles on him in 1905, 1908, and 1914. He lectured frequently and his writings were widely circulated in America. But it was in Europe, particularly Germany and Holland, that he had his greatest influence. He published a set of drawings and later a book of writings and photographs through the Berlin firm of Wasmuth, which brought him fame in Europe as well as the attention of such key proto-Modern architects as Peter Behrens. Dutch architects immersed themselves in his work, going so far in one or two cases as to build almost literal copies of his houses in Holland.

Interestingly, his influence was deflected by the split between Dutch de Stijl architects, who represented Rationalism, Functionalism, and the forthcoming International Style, and the *Wendingen* group, named for the architectural journal, which included most of the architects that have customarily been called Expressionist. *Wendingen* even devoted a special issue to Wright and thus he became identified in Europe with a school whose influence was soon to disappear in favor of the International Style.

Le Corbusier's audience was the circle of artists and intellectuals at the core of the avant-garde in Paris. He gained attention by founding, as a painter and along with another painter, Ozenfant, the Purist movement, a sort of post facto Cubism. He published and wrote for a magazine, *L'Ésprit Nouveau,* which was widely circulated during its years of publication (1920–22), and wrote a series of books, the most influential of which, *Vers Une Architecture,* was approvingly reviewed by no less than Wright himself, as has been mentioned previously.[30] He also exhibited his work, most memorably in the Pavillon de l'Ésprit Nouveau at the Exposition Internationale des Arts Décoratifs in Paris in 1925 and at the Weissenhof exhibition of 1927 at Stuttgart, where Ludwig Mies van der Rohe, who was in charge of the exhibition, gave him first choice of sites.

Rejection by the Establishment: Retrenchment

Both Wright and Le Corbusier decided early in their careers not to take the conventional paths to success that had been offered to them. Instead, they developed their revolutionary architectures through a combination of relentless perseverance and masterful public relations. They each advanced far enough in about ten years from the invention of prototypes to produce culminating masterpieces that received international attention. But just at this point, each was blocked from further development by the rejection of a major project. They both drastically curtailed their architectural production and began long periods of reevaluation of their initial philosophies.

For Wright, the rejection of his proposed house for the McCormicks (1908) meant the loss of access to clients with the greatest means for building large architectural projects. A success with the McCormick House would have meant acceptance by the businessmen of downtown Chicago. Wright could not have been unaware of the volume of construction going on in the Loop while he was building houses in Oak Park, not to mention the grand schemes of the "City Beautiful" Chicago Plan of 1906. He refused to continue at the scale of Oak Park and his elopement to Europe with Mrs. Cheney in 1909 was a slap of defiance in the face of those who had refused him admittance to their circles.

There followed twenty years of turmoil in his life. The projects of this period are remarkable for variety and experimentation. He revolutionized his own methods of planning and building houses with his concrete block system developed for the conditions particular to California. The Midway Gardens (Chicago, 1913) were an advance in abstraction of form. The National Life Insurance (Chicago) and St. Mark's Tower (New York) projects of 1924 and 1929, respectively, represented a virtual redefinition of the skyscraper away from the steel cage frame and toward a cantilevered structural system, which Wright believed was more suited to reinforced concrete construction. He directed his attention toward planning, perhaps in response to Le Corbusier's *Vers Une Architecture,* inventing a sort of working suburban utopia called Broadacre City, and started his own

architecture school, the Taliesin Foundation, perhaps in response to Walter Gropius's Bauhaus at Dessau. But all of this was done in the face of criticial disregard; very little of anything was built.

Le Corbusier's retrenchment began with the rejection of his proposed scheme for the League of Nations Headquarters. His very advanced project, although widely admired in avant-garde circles, succumbed in favor of a late Beaux-Arts scheme of remarkable mediocrity. When, in response to a change of site, this winning project was revised to resemble (in plan if not in style) his own rejected entry, Le Corbusier was devastated. The years of reduced output that followed, through the 1930s and World War II, have been discussed in connection with the 1932 Museum of Modern Art show.

Late Careers: Renascence

Nothing sets Wright and Le Corbusier further apart from other twentieth-century architects than the phenomena of their late careers. The years of public rejection and resistance to their ideas were to be a time of reassessment and renewal for them. The works that each produced in his later years are distinguished by a fluency of construction and depth of meaning that to a great extent surpass the capability of verbal analysis. Exasperated by the ineffable quality of these works, most critics have resorted to rhetoric or poetry in the case of Le Corbusier and have more or less ignored the late career of Wright.

It has been shown previously that the basis of the first works of Wright's resurgence in the late 1930s was his response to the International Style and, in particular, to the Villa Savoie. Although the new (for him) emphasis on structural members seems to be the result of direct influence, much of the other characteristics of these late works—the more clearly expressed geometry, the smoother surfaces, the tighter planning grids—had been developing in his California houses of the 1920s. His reaction to the general identification of the International Style with Modern architecture, then, was not so much a striking out against the International Style as a claim for common roots between his work and that of the Europeans. The buildings of Wright's last twenty years demonstrate an incredibly wide range of styles. There are Prairie houses under sheltering roofs, but now these have an economy of detail and directness of treatment that overcome the fussiness of some of the earlier houses. They are matched—sometimes even neighbored, as in Pleasantville, New York—by new types of houses based on circular or angular plans that in planning and execution made contemporary houses seem timid. Most important of these new types, of course, is the basic Usonian, an easily built, beautifully detailed but essentially modest small house meant for the average American family of the middle twentieth century. At the end of this period, just before Wright's death at ninety-two, come the real masterpieces such as the Guggenheim Museum in New York, the Beth Sholom Synagogue in Philadelphia, or the Marin County Civic Center in San Rafael, California, works that still challenge the ability of critics to explain them adequately.

Le Corbusier's resurgence after World War II was characterized, as has been mentioned, by the complex shapes of organic growth rather than the simple forms of Cartesian geometry that he had previously favored. The smooth, neutral, white surfaces of his 1920s houses—which had deteriorated partly because of his eschewal of the edges and drip moldings necessary for protecting the surfaces from weather—were abandoned in favor of the natural appearance of rough concrete, *béton brut*, fresh from the formwork. The Cartesian grid, which had determined his plans before 1930, was replaced by the Modulor, a system of proportionally increasing increments that is based on the Fibonacci series, a mathematical principle that has been demonstrated to occur frequently in nature. Flat roof planes became curved parasols or cisterns and thin facades thickened in response to sun and weather circumstances. Yet the continuity between his later period and his earlier work is undeniable; like Wright, Le Corbusier was not reacting against any particular theory so much as he was extending the validity of earlier principles to a larger domain of activity. Each architect's late career, then, is a demonstration of the mutual application of generalized principles of Modern architecture to the work of both.

The historical similarities between the careers of Wright and Le Corbusier can be augmented by a comparison of certain theoretical principles that they appear to have held more or less in common. These are Le Corbusier's "Five Points of a New Architecture" and Wright's "Five Resources for Modern Architecture."

Le Corbusier's Five Points were first elucidated in 1927 in connection with a publication on the Weissenhof exhibition in Stuttgart. This was also the year in which his *Vers Une Architecture* was published in translation and reviewed by Wright. The Five Points were interpreted by most critics as a definitive statement of what would soon be named the International Style. Each Point names a particular aspect of Le Corbusier's buildings that intentionally contributes to his definition of a new architecture.

The first Point, *pilotis,* represented the basis for

Le Corbusier's break with the past. *Pilotis* referred to the array of identical supporting posts on a Cartesian grid plan that could generate a mass-produced construction system. Their simple cylindrical section could be varied to express unusual load or circulation conditions. Furthermore, in lifting the building above the site, they allowed for a simplified foundation of easily made point supports beneath the grid, which enabled the designer to adapt the system economically to different sites. Thus, the *pilotis* were the basis for a functional and structural system with a legitimate claim to universal applicability.

As used by Le Corbusier, however, the system became more esthetically expressive than structurally inevitable. In fact, his Dom-Ino system—which was the theoretical predecessor to the Five Points and which was also based on *piloti* supports—is structurally unstable as designed because it lacks resistance to lateral forces. It needs reinforcement from segments of solid wall in both axial directions, either at the perimeter or somewhere within, to resist horizontal forces such as wind. But from an esthetic and functional standpoint, the *pilotis* were the most important of the Five Points.

The second Point was the *roof garden*. Le Corbusier seemed to offer this amenity to make up for the separation of building from site implied by the *pilotis*. Historically, it certainly has had the least importance of any of the Points for the development of the International Style. But it sums up Le Corbusier's ambivalent attitude toward nature in providing a private, contemplative environment for experiencing light and air, allowing only for such plants as can survive on a terrace. Although in practice Le Corbusier recommended cultivating whatever wild seeds the winds happened to bring to his planting beds, he made use of freestanding canopy roofs

and wall segments to increase the control of the architectural continuum over the natural.

The *free plan* was, after *pilotis,* the second most important Point. It allowed for a building to be designed around movement rather than stasis and created the dynamic quality that would distinguish the new architecture from the old. It also provided flexibility in the placement of partitions that bear no load and therefore encouraged the standardization of a building type that can be applied in many different situations. Ultimately, the free plan probably derived from Wright's German publications and was one of the basic similarities between the two architects.

The fourth Point, the *ribbon window*, had the character both of universal idea and personal taste. In simplest terms, Le Corbusier wished to allow light into his buildings while maintaining control over the view. The ribbon windows were meant to represent the independence of fenestration from the other building elements, but a total glass facade, such as the one he used at the Cité du Réfuge in Paris, would have been a more general case of this. The ribbon window, therefore, was really a means of articulating his otherwise blank white facades. In this sense it was an attempt to use windows decoratively and, again, it was a motif used earlier by Wright.

The final Point, the *free facade*, once again expressed a personal esthetic choice. When structure is organized around a clearly defined system of *pilotis* and the windows are regularized in a separate system, the hierarchy typical of a Classical facade is destroyed. Permitting the exterior walls to act merely as a system of screens, as light containers of the forces within that can be punctured, fractured, or translated in response to the other systems, introduces a new dynamic and unpredictable arrangement of facade elements. Although presented by Le Corbusier as a functional consideration, the free facade is most important as a component of an esthetic that celebrates the intersection of coordinated systems in space.

Le Corbusier's Five Points, then, have a twofold importance. At the literal level, they offer the best, most concise definition of the International Style as it was around 1930. But more important is their assertion of an esthetic appropriate to an architecture based, as both Wright and Le Corbusier demanded, on the *standardization of elements*. Le Corbusier's description of a *system* of supports, a *system* of fenestration and a plan reflecting a *system* of circulation, each determined independently according to appropriate functional and technical criteria, is the first instance of the verbal expression of what was to characterize a truly *Modern* architecture. In allowing these systems to remain visually independent, to intersect and overlap and cancel each other out according to the circumstances of function or construction, Le Corbusier made manifest in his works of the 1920s the clearest statement up to that time of what the twentieth-century environment would be like.

Meanwhile, Wright in his California houses of the 1920s had been approaching a similar consciousness of independent systems. His "Five Resources for Modern Architecture," written for his 1932 autobiography and excerpted for the Museum of Modern Art exhibition catalog, stands as an interesting comparison to Le Corbusier's Five Points. Unlike the latter, Wright's cannot be read as a description of a particular building; they are more general in meaning. But like the Five Points, they propose functional considerations that generate a series of independent *systems* of building elements.

The first Resource is "*the sense of the within—Space—as Reality.*"[31] Analogous to Le Corbusier's third Point, the free plan, it referred to the significance of the interior room as the form generator for the overall building. It also called for the integration of interior with exterior into a comprehensive unified space. Furthermore, it expressed the unity of form and function in that the room was considered to be a *place* whose form was determined by a particular *activity*. At the deepest level, it meant that the essence of the Organic is the natural: that is, that the forms of organic beings are the result of natural forces. This was to be incorporated into architecture by allowing the forces identified as determining the place-to-be to be symbolically made manifest in the space-that-is. The other four Resources were instruments to effect this first and greatest Resource, which in itself encompassed the "one great new integrity."

The essence of Wright's agreement with the principles of Le Corbusier is his definition of form as a direct result of a specific and identifiable force or forces. Interpreted in the light of his earlier assertion that style is to be achieved through standardization (see chapter 1), the first Resource implies the separation of building elements into coordinated, independent systems. It is not surprising, then, to find that the other four Resources begin to define these systems and how they are to be manipulated.

The second Resource is *glass*. Instead of the ribbon window of Le Corbusier's second Point, Wright focuses on the nature of the material itself. He sees it as "air in air to keep air out or keep it in."[32] It supports his idea of a building growing from the earth toward light in emulation of what he saw as the archetypal embodiment of natural process, the tree.

The third Resource is *continuity*. Like Le Corbusier's Point about the *piloti*, it celebrates reinforced concrete, but there is an important technical difference. Wright considered the steel reinforcing within the concrete as the essence of the system. He describes this essence as "tenuity"[33] or the ability of the steel to resist tension. Thus, plasticity of form, smooth transitions from member to member in gentle angles or curves, is favored over the abrupt articulation of structural parts characteristic of the International Style. Where Le Corbusier stressed the independent character of mass-produced structural parts assembled in the field, Wright believed that the true nature of factory production would be found in the variety of steel meshes and rods that could be easily modeled at the site to support thin, light shells and planes of concrete. Continuity as a Resource, then, is the kernel of his disagreement with Le Corbusier about the nature of mass production.

The fourth Resource is an *understanding of the nature of materials.* Where Le Corbusier emphasized the forms imposed upon standardized parts by machine processes—for example, the smooth, abstract cylinder of the *piloti*—Wright supported any particular and personal manipulation that the architect might use to adapt the inherent qualities of a building material to a given use. He stressed the differences between the various materials available to the modern architect. His smooth, white stucco surfaces, unlike those of Le Corbusier, were used in his early work to differentiate a wall panel from a dark-stained wood surround.

The fifth Resource is *pattern as natural—integral ornament.* Denying applied decoration, this Resource emphasizes the selection of finishes and details that will elucidate upon the larger-scale elements of the building. Wright felt that the "plain, flat surfaces" of the International Style, "cut to shape for its own sake," become "no less ornamental than egg-and-dart . . . the moment it is sophisticatedly placed."[34] And yet there is a note, if not approval, of at least tolerance: " 'The machine for living in' is sterile, but therefore safer, I believe, than the festering mass of ancient styles or imitation organic."[35]

In comparing the careers and theoretical writings of Wright and Le Corbusier, one is struck by the correspondences. Especially around 1930, at the time of greatest similarity between them, there are only two significant differences in their theories: the appropriate relation between man and nature and the proper expression of modern construction methods. While these differences will be more fully explored later on, the following examination of the complexity of their work will show the danger of too lightly accepting simplistic theories about their contrasting style. For it is only through acknowledging the profundity of a common meaning in their work that Wright and Le Corbusier may be seen as savants for Modern architects.

4 Wright and Le Corbusier as Savants:
Problems in Style and Theme

There is need for an approach that coordinates the roles of both Wright and Le Corbusier as savants of Modern architecture. It has so far been characteristic of most twentieth-century criticism that one or the other of the two is presented as the sole founder of Modern architecture, which in itself is testimony to the importance of their work. But with this tendency to appoint a single source for Modernism, there is a consequent dismissal of the other, a rationalistic tidying up around the edges of theory that is no substitute at all for an honest and unprejudiced appraisal of *both* men. It is far beyond the scope of this analysis to document the attitude of *every* important critic on this issue; it will suffice to mention some of the more common assumptions that have been too readily accepted as true.

At the core of these attitudes is the notion that Wright's work is personal and individual, whereas Le Corbusier's is general and archetypal. This seems to explain the apparent lack of direct influence by Wright on Modern architecture as opposed to the profusion of buildings that resemble Le Corbusier's early style. It is a charge often made against such architects as Gaudí and Aalto and even broadly

used, in the term *expressionism,* against whole groups of architects who have dared to deviate from the most superficial resemblance of their work to that of others. Such an attitude is blind to a procedure whose goal is to find deep correspondences between buildings that need not look very much alike on the surface.

Connected with this is the idea that Wright's architecture is subjective whereas Le Corbusier's is objective. Wright's buildings are often called warm or emotional where Le Corbusier's are cool or rational. Expressed in this manner, such opinions seem to be based on an observer's immediate impressions rather than on clear and unprejudiced observation.

There are other contrasts made, however, that indeed seem to identify key distinctions between Wright and Le Corbusier. Wright's work is often seen as handcrafted, in contrast to the machine fabrication characteristic of Le Corbusier. Reyner Banham has pointed out,[36] in reference to Wright's influence in Holland after World War I, the degree to which Wright's work, too, supports an interpretation of a machine esthetic. But it is certainly fair to say that, in contrast to Le Corbusier, Wright believed that modern machines would increase the influence of the craftsman; he invented in his Usonian houses a simplified means of construction with which fine detailing and joinery of wooden elements could be achieved by semiskilled laborers using sophisticated portable machine tools. This is quite different from Le Corbusier's ideal of finishes achieved at the factory, leaving only a sort of assemblage to be done at the site.

It is important to point out that both architects were really referring to "the art of the machined" rather than "the art of the machine." In their early careers, they selected certain industrial processes, such as extrusion, planing, and cutting, in favor of others, for example, casting and molding, as representative of modern finishing techniques. It would be difficult to justify such choices on the basis of function or technology alone. Casting and molding are of prime importance in such essentially modern materials as glass and concrete and therefore must be as relevant to an industrial age as the other processes mentioned. And, in retrospect, it seems pointless to have attempted smooth, polished surfaces on poured concrete, wood, and stone, which are by their natures very different from metal and glass. In fact, both architects abandoned their early prejudices against the qualities associated with casting in the rendered and patterned masonry surfaces of their later careers. Thus, "machine art," for all its Rationalist and Functionalist implications, is finally no more than an esthetic stance, justifiable only from a formal point of view.

Another important contrast between the two architects is that Wright was nature oriented whereas Le Corbusier was city oriented. It has turned out historically that the enormous increase in population experienced by the West in this century resulted in two phenomena: the dispersal of population throughout formerly rural areas (suburbanization) and the concentration of population in high-density cities (urbanization). Each architect foresaw one of these trends. Wright's interest in the family led him to promote suburbanization through his Broadacre City, and Le Corbusier's involvement with larger communal units (the monastery at Ema and the community of avant-garde artists in Paris around 1915) naturally predisposed him toward La Ville Radieuse and other urban schemes. The concentration of intellectuals in cities, particularly in Europe, has influenced critics to favor the urban view and, in the case of certain writers such as Benevolo and Tafuri, has created a blind spot to much of Wright's work. But it cannot be said today that one tendency has finally emerged as dominant. Both suburbanization and urbanization are continuing forces in the late twentieth century and relevance cannot reasonably be denied either Wright or Le Corbusier on the grounds of their advocating either.

This brings up a third justifiable contrast between the two. Wright is essentially American whereas Le Corbusier is European. This, of course, flies in the faces of those who assert that the International Style is universally applicable and deny the uniqueness of the American situation. But the way that America has developed, i.e., as an untouched pool of natural resources ready to be put to use by an industrializing culture from Europe, is perhaps more pertinent to housing the masses of today's world than is the historical development of Europe, a gradual and empirical attempt to extend control over its environment by the resident culture. Wright considered himself to be the natural successor to Jefferson, Emerson, and Thoreau and believed in the American experience as a modern replacement of the old civilizations of Europe. What is interesting is that Le Corbusier's urban vision was realized earlier in

America than it was in Europe, whereas the centrally planned garden suburbs of early twentieth-century England were more advanced in planning than were those in America of the same period. Notwithstanding that the American nations are essentially branches of older Western societies with slight admixtures of the native culture, the question is how much the experience of Western civilization in the Americas has changed the course of that civilization itself, and how much the Europeans are willing to see themselves as changed by the American phenomenon. It is on this that the relative importance of Wright's Americanism and Le Corbusier's Europeanism hinges.

In looking beyond these contrasts, commonly taken for granted, problems arise in trying to define the purported stylistic divergence of Wright and Le Corbusier, or the Organic and the International Styles (which is saying the same thing, at least before 1935). Historians have been reluctant to suggest distinctive characteristics that would encapsulate their work, particularly in the case of Wright. In his short but thoughtful monograph on Wright, Vincent Scully,[37] although he shies away from defining a style, gives three themes that are both important and consistent in Wright's work. These are (1) abstraction of function and geometry, (2) expression of interior space through massing, and (3) integrity of structure with expression. Consider in comparison the three characteristics of the International Style given by Hitchcock and Johnson[38]: (1) emphasis upon volume—space enclosed by thin planes or surfaces as opposed to the suggestion of mass and solidity, (2) regularity as opposed to symmetry or other kinds of obvious balance, and (3) dependence on intrinsic elegance of materials, technical perfection, and fine proportions, as opposed to applied ornament.

The first points—Wright's abstraction of function and geometry, also referred to as continuity of space, and Le Corbusier's emphasis upon volume—seem to refer more or less to the same characteristic. Abstraction of function and geometry, a favorite concept of theoreticians in this century, refers to the suppression of small-scale differentiation and detailing in favor of simplified large-scale elements that directly represent a vision of the functional configuration of the building. The emphasis upon volume amounts to the same thing: thin planes and surfaces simply rendered to reflect the space within, shaped according to functional needs. Scully's second point on Wright—the expression of interior space through massing—contradicts the first point of the International Style only in that the latter provides a precise definition of mass wheras Scully uses the term more loosely: His "expression of interior space" is quite the same as Hitchcock and Johnson's "emphasis upon volume."

Scully's third point—the integrity of structure in Wright's work—is related although not identical to Hitchcock and Johnson's second and third: regularity and the dependence upon intrinsic quality in materials. The common thread here is the integrity of structural elements as a system, something that has been discussed in chapter 2. Allowing structure to have visible independence, to be read as a coherent system not deriving from the other building elements, is to endow it with integrity, as Scully requires, and with regularity as opposed to a forced symmetry or balance, as Hitchcock and Johnson demand. The expression of an intrinsic quality of a material in opposition to an applied ornament or finish has always been claimed for both Organic architecture and the International Style.

It would not be to the point to try to develop the stylistic definitions given above as examples. They are too vague to do justice to the work of Wright and Le Corbusier. It is important to bring out, however, that Scully, Hitchcock, and Johnson seem to be defining the work of the two architects in quite a similar manner, although this was surely not their intention. It must be emphasized as well that the impression of a sharp distinction between Wright and Le Corbusier, discernible in these as in almost all other treatments of twentieth-century architecture, is derived not from a clear definition of style but from unspoken judgments transmitted to the reader in subtle ways.

One difficulty in trying to distill stylistic differences between Wright and Le Corbusier is that a variety of styles can be detected in each architect's work. A comparison of Wright's Robie House (Chicago, 1906) with his Ennis House (Los Angeles, 1923) is apropos since both were of similar size, built on constricted sites. The two houses share an emphasized longitudinal continuity, the long row of casement windows and French doors on the main living floor of the Robie House becoming the colonnaded gallery of the more developed Ennis House (figs. 4-1 and 4-2). Entry in both houses is by stairs that rise next to the dining room and give on to a circulation gallery past the fireplace to the living room. But the fenestration is different. The continuous ribbon windows of the Robie House contrast with the isolated glass lites of the Ennis House, located at the centers of walls and at the corners of rooms. The great height of the ceilings inside the Ennis House is opposed to the low Prairie roofs of the Robie House.

The change in material from the brick of the Robie House to the concrete block of the Ennis House is the most overt manifestation of a subtle but important change in style. The concrete blocks are not masonry units per se, but are part of a stressed skin system that Wright called *textile block*

4-1. Wright: Robie House, Hyde Park, Illinois, 1906.

because of its woven, fabriclike nature. The continuous steel reinforcing strands along the horizontal and vertical joints of the blocks allow the walls to become either pierced screens, integrally supported masses, or structural frames around glass doors and windows without any change in the detailing of the system. Therefore, the three-part system of the Robie House—brick wall masses, wood-and-glass ribbon windows, and overhanging roofs—is transformed at the Ennis House to a single material used in three different ways (figs. 4-3 and 4-4). Screen walls are differentiated from structural frames by the slope of the former contrasting with the plumb orientation of the latter. Openings are made by simply dropping blocks out. Thus the Prairie style, characterized by differentiating systems of elements with a change of materials, is replaced in the Ennis House by a

4-2. Wright: Ennis House, Los Angeles, 1923.

4-3. Wright: Robie House.

4-4. Wright: Ennis House.

Ozenfant (Paris, 1922) with his Maison Week-end (Paris, 1935) reveals a basic similarity in the free disposition of functional areas and the direct relation of the fenestration to these areas. But the construction elements of each house are entirely different. The Maison Ozenfant is based on Le Corbusier's Dom-Ino system, a straightforward concrete slab-and-column frame enclosed by light screen walls. As mentioned earlier in connection with the Villa Savoie, it is the interaction of the fenestration system with the walls and freestanding structure that creates the special esthetic quality of this type of house. Maison Week-end, on the other hand, is built of arched concrete vaults supported on longitudinal masonry walls. Glass block is used for much of the fenestration in recognition of the load-bearing nature of these walls. The ribbon window would not be appropriate to this vocabulary and it is replaced by isolated units of glass interrupting the supporting walls. The vaults pass over these openings without responding to the change in support. It is a system not dissimilar to that of the Robie House, excepting, of course, that the latter uses ribbon windows. As with Wright, Le Corbusier is found to have changed not just his palette of materials but the natures of the systems of building elements as well.

The range of stylistic variety common to both Wright's and Le Corbusier's work that has just been demonstrated can cause problems for critical analysis. Although it may at first seem to be quite the opposite case, the critical challenge is exacerbated by the continuity of certain themes throughout all the variants of style. For, in order to take account of the profundity of meaning in these great architects' buildings, the critic must demonstrate the links between the styles, as well as identify them individually. Pending more lengthy analysis, two examples may be presented here; each can be interpreted as an organization of

more subtle manipulation of a single, flexible building technique, the particular configuration of which defines the structure/screen/opening functions of the walls of the house. Wright's development of his new vocabulary can be traced through the Barnsdall House (Los Angeles, 1917–21), which begins to expand the use of a smoothly rendered flat wall beyond the Prairie style while retaining certain aspects of Prairie fenestration and low ceilings (fig. 4-5), and through the three intermediate block houses in Hollywood and Pasadena, which experiment with the textile block system but without the slanting planes of Barnsdall.

Stylistic multiplicity can also be found in Le Corbusier's early work. A comparison of the Maison certain building elements into coordinated, independent systems.

The first theme is *the expressed separation of structure and screen*. Wright began to develop this theme in his Prairie houses. Where the wood-and-glass window system was opposed to brick masses, as at the D. D. Martin and Robie houses, a simple change of materials served to distinguish the brick structural piers from the wooden screen partitions. But in the stucco-veneered houses, the dichotomy between stuccoed supporting piers and stuccoed screens was more difficult to express. Wright experimented with reveals, patterns of boards, and returned corners thoughout the Prairie years and his perseverance indicates his anticipation of a more profound statement of this theme to come. To move from the distinction of building systems (mass, window wall, and roof) by material (brick, wood-and-glass, and tile) toward a distinction between the *issue* of materials and the *issue* of building elements, consequently enhancing the independence of systems and enriching the potential for meaning, was for Wright an act of the greatest significance. The Barnsdall House is his first attempt to distinguish supporting elements from screening elements by tilting the latter slightly from the perpendicular. Seven years later, in the Ennis House, this configuration is perfected in the battering of the block walls through controlled offsets in successive courses. Although he used the material-specific defining method on many occasions throughout his career, the more developed approach—ordering systems of building elements according to their orientation to the vertical—appears in many of the Usonian houses, most of the skyscraper projects, and the Beth Sholom Synagogue, Guggenheim Museum, and other late masterpieces.

Le Corbusier's work explores the same theme,

4-5. Wright: Barnsdall House, Los Angeles, 1917.

as has been extensively pointed out by many critics. In fact, one of his Five Points, the free facade, is an explicit manifestation of the separation of structure from screen. As with Wright, his involvement deepened over the years and his handling of the theme is much more subtle and moving in his later buildings. Starting with the Dom-Ino system of the early houses, Le Corbusier treated the separation of columns from walls in a very straightforward manner: The lines of his partitions did not coincide with structural elements. The limitations of this approach became apparent when, for economic and functional reasons, the columns had to be engaged in the walls. Also, the offsetting of partitions by several inches from a line of columns could only be read from one side of the partition. In the Cité du Réfuge and Pavillon Suisse of the early 1930s, Le Corbusier can be discerned struggling with these problems. His use of curved surfaces, either geometric or free-form, offered a solution, and such late masterpieces as Ronchamp, La Tourette, the Visual Arts Center at Harvard, and the buildings of Chandigarh all exhibit profound contrasts between flat and curved surfaces that can be read as subtle comments on the distinction between supporting and screening elements.

The other important twentieth-century theme to be discussed is *the identification of the circulation path as an independent system within the functional continuum of a building.* Recognition of the importance of circulation can, of course, be traced back to the beginnings of architecture itself. It is rather the consciousness of the circulation function as an *independent* act having a meaning apart from the other building elements that is a characteristic concern of the twentieth-century.

Wright in his Prairie period became interested in this theme as an aspect of the extension of interior space into the outdoors. At the D. D. Martin House, the gallery between the main house and the remote conservatory could be seen from the entry as a path deeply penetrating through the house and out again into the garden. But the gallery and house were treated as distinct elements. By the time of the Robie House, the colonnade of brick piers along the street side of the main living floor implied a circulation gallery incorporated into the house itself. The theme matured in the Ennis House, where the colonnaded walk was allowed to stretch the full length of the site, connecting interior living spaces and exterior terraces with a minimum of modification. The revolutionary zoning of this house—the complete isolation of four bedroom suites separated by open-plan common living areas—reinforced the colonnade as a path between places. After the 1920s, the path became a major feature in much of Wright's work, manifesting itself as bridges (the Johnson Wax Headquarters, the Marin County Civic Center) or as covered walkways (Fallingwater, Florida Southern College). At the Guggenheim Museum, the path is both of these and more: It has become the generating element of the architectural totality.

There is a similar development of the circulation path throughout the career of Le Corbusier. First encountered as an appendage at the entrance to his Maison Citrohan prototype, the path appeared as a freestanding bridge (at the villa built at Vaucresson in 1922), as a tiny balcony extending the interior circulation through the external wall at the Maison Cook in Paris, and as freestanding stairways at the Villa Stein and Maison Planex. The path could be as subtle as an interior corridor with gently curving side walls or as explicit as the curving ramp in the main studio of the Maison La Roche. The culminating experiment was the Villa Savoie, where the ramp became strong enough to become an independent element, affecting the other parts of the house as much as they impinged on it. Le Corbusier began to express the act of circulating by shaping other building elements as if they had actually reacted to being struck by an invisible moving force. Thus the entry sequence at the Cité du Réfuge in Paris includes penetrating and slicing off two sides of the cube at the top of the stairs as well as being deflected to the right from the vividly colored interior wall. Structural columns swell and contract in response to the implied movement. This is a theme much favored by Le Corbusier and can be seen very subtly employed in the Pavillon Suisse as well.

By the time of his late masterpieces, Le Corbusier could generate complex and subtle circulation patterns in his buildings, depending for their effect on a modulation of the independence of the path as system. At the Visual Arts Center at Harvard University, it is left ambiguous whether the double-ended ramp has been twisted into an S by the building or the building itself has been twisted askew by the turning of the ramp. At the monastery of La Tourette, the crossed central corridors offer circulation independent of the cloisterlike hallways attached to the interior walls of the surrounding blocks. The ramp at the entry to the High Court at Chandigarh is as strong and independent an element as the ranked courtrooms to the right.

All of this indicates that style and content are to some extent independent of each other in the work of Frank Lloyd Wright and Le Corbusier. It would be pointless to try to define a Wrightian or Corbusian "style," since each of them mastered several styles and often used them simultaneously. It may be suspected, too, that if the development of Modernism is more than the invention of a particular style, the foundations of Modernism lie very deep. It has already been demonstrated that the organization of building elements into coordinated independent systems can be the basis for a Modern concept of style. Both Wright and Le Corbusier used this interplay as their prime expressive technique. Themes of vital importance in the Modern world can be found in the work of each. The independence of structure from screen and the manifestation of circulation as path are only two of these; more could certainly be found. But the greater question is why? What is it about contemporary experience that makes these themes relevant? Since so much has been revealed from an admittedly casual comparison of this century's two greatest architects, a more comprehensive evaluation may be expected to offer material suitable for founding a theory of Modern architecture.

5 Wright and Le Corbusier as Exemplars:
Deriving a Critical Approach

It is not surprising that today an interest in Classicism has sprung up among those architects who most strongly reject the tenets of International Style Modernism. For at the time when Wright and Le Corbusier were establishing the parameters of a new order, Classicism in Beaux-Arts guise was still around as the most potent architectural movement since the Renaissance. It was not the human-scaled and nature-oriented architecture of the Greeks, but rather the grandiloquent Imperial Classicism of the Romans that held sway among fashionable architects in Europe and America around the turn of the century. This interpretation of Classicism depends for much of its persuasive power on the length of its pedigree, demonstrating a uniquely hallowed cultural connection with ancient times. For the purposes of this analysis, the most important aspect of Classicism is its advocacy of a single, hierarchically ordered architectural continuum, a unified and perfectly lucid system of building elements adaptable, in theory at least, to any building type. By historical chance, Classical theory came to depend heavily upon the interpretations made by writers over the centuries of a single ancient treatise on architecture, that of the Roman architect Vitruvius.

Vitruvian analysis defines three determinants of an architectural problem: *venustas* or form, *utilitas* or function, and *firmitas* or building technology. Evaluation of a work of architecture is to be made with regard to these three in order to reach a fair assessment. In the twentieth century, many critics—most notably Christian Norberg-Schulz in his *Intentions in Architecture*—have identified a fourth determinant to account for the relation of symbolic and archetypal elements of architecture to the larger culture in a historical sense. This has been referred to as the *iconographic* element, and it addresses itself to the user of the building as representative of the culture at large. Such first-rate writers as Norberg-Schulz and Robert Venturi have focused on this fourth element, seeing here great potential for a more comprehensive interpretation of architecture. The distinction between communication at the formal and iconographic levels is that the former looks at extracultural meanings and universal values whereas the latter considers intracultural meanings and local values.

In the simplest terms, the iconographic interpretation of architecture addresses the quality of the architectural object as a communications medium.

Charles Jencks has defined "a failure of modern architecture" to be one of "communication,"[39] and it is precisely this element that most clearly exhibits the divergence of the thinking of both Wright and Le Corbusier from early-twentieth-century criticism. Since this debate took place within the Vitruvian schema, the modified, four-determinant Vitruvian approach can be developed to seek legitimate standards for comparing Wright and Le Corbusier in their early careers.

Form

One major distinction often proposed about architecture in the twentieth century is *clarity of mass*. This is what seems to have been meant by references to "pure form," "simple geometric shapes," and so forth. On the surface, the connection appears obvious, but it must not be accepted too readily. It can be seen that in almost every historical period of a culture advanced enough to produce relatively large, monumental buildings, there has been a tendency toward clarity of mass. The pyramids and pylon entries of the Egyptians, the Greek temple, the Romanesque church, the Gothic cathedral, the Renaissance palazzo, and the Beaux-Arts office building all incorporate in some sense the idea of clarity of mass. There are different ways to interpret the term, of course, and the changes in meaning from one historical period to another can be good delineators of major changes in style.

The clarity of mass concept is often carried to the extreme of demands for Platonic solids in design: the cube, sphere, cylinder, and cone. In practice, of course, these shapes vary tremendously in their applicability within the constraints of function and construction. What is ineffable in geometry can too easily become unspeakable in architecture.

Another interpretation of clarity of mass has to do with the eschewal of ornament. The distinction between that which is ornamental and that which is substantial can be difficult to make. One could cite Borromini, for example, whose door and window frames can be read as discourses on the relation between ornament and structure. In his work, the structure often seems to twist in response to the pressure of ostensibly minor elements.

For the Neoclassical architects of the late eighteenth and early nineteenth centuries, a lack of ornament meant freeing the archeologically correct Classical Greek or Roman orders from any other applied elements. But the designers of the early twentieth century wanted to clear away the orders themselves. Auguste Perret, Le Corbusier's mentor, reduced building elements to functional parts of simplified profile such as cornices, frames, and drip moldings. Le Corbusier divested his early work of even these parts, much to the detriment of their weathering abilities.

Since the concept of clarity of mass has been applied so variously in the past, it should be refined in recognition of its twentieth-century manifestation. It is proposed, therefore, that today clarity of mass means above all else *integrity of the surfaces and edges of underlying masses*. For Le Corbusier, this has meant suppressing all frames, moldings, minor edges, and reveals from the walls of his buildings. For Wright, it involves an expression of mass independent of the ornamental system.

A second aspect of form that is characteristic of twentieth-century architecture is the *Cartesian planning grid*. Ideally, the grid is formed by the intersection of two sets of equidistant parallel lines at right angles. An early manifestation of this in architecture is the primitive hypostyle hall characteristic of some ancient architectures. The presence of the column is dramatically enhanced in such halls, the multitudinous repetition evoking a sense of congregation even when the hall is empty. It is this intensity that Wright expresses in the Johnson Wax Headquarters, as pointed out by Norris Kelly Smith in his book on Wright.[40] But at a deeper level, the developed Cartesian grid can produce the opposite feeling by diminishing the size and importance of the columns until they become the intersections of a series of parallel transparent planes that divide the building into cubic spatial cells. The modern concept of phenomenal transparency is related to this.[41]

Although the expression of a series of spatial cells can be seen in the Cistercian monasteries of the Middle Ages and by way of Brunelleschi in the early Renaissance, for instance, perhaps the most extreme Neoclassical example was at Versailles, where Hardouin-Mansart at the end of the seventeenth century acknowledged the imperial ambitions of Louis XIV by building parts of the main palace and the Grand Trianon as immensely long blocks of replicated bays. The expanse of these works is much stronger than the more typically baroque emphasis on the center bays. It was with the changes in construction methods and materials of the nineteenth century—the most striking example being the Crystal Palace—that this quality of the Cartesian planning grid began to be explored again for its own sake, representing the repetitive nature of mass assembly for those architects who sought an expression of modern production. Thus, it can be said that for the Cartesian planning grid in the twentieth century, it is the spaces rather than the columns that are of the essence, the *generation of a series of spatial cells from a system of perpendicular transparent planes.*

Clearly defined masses arranged according to a Cartesian grid are characteristic of many architectural periods other than the modern. But a distinctively Modern quality can be discerned in how the masses are assembled. In architectures of the past, the masses tend to be congruent with the grid, producing a strict hierarchical order among the constituent parts. Even where actual misalignments are made, the purpose is still to present a perceivably unified plan. But in the twentieth century, architects have become interested in arranging forms on a grid in such a way that both grid and mass assemblage retain some independence. This may be discerned in some of Wright's later plan drawings where the walls follow the centerlines of the grid squares rather than the grid lines themselves. Barry Maitland's article, "The Grid,"[42] demonstrates how Le Corbusier's early buildings were based on an interplay between the circulation, the defining walls, and the structural grid. Each in some way determines the others, but none is overridingly dominant. Different things seem to occupy the same space at the same time, resulting in that sort of charged space characteristic of twentieth-century architecture. This concept of independence of plan and mass will be developed later as one of the two key ideas in defining Modern architecture, but for now, as a purely formal characteristic, it will be called *disjuncture.*

Another characteristic of the way forms are put together in the twentieth century can be called *dynamic balance.* Some theoreticians identify this with asymmetry, but the latter is really a special case. Dynamic balance means more than asymmetry; it has great importance to Modern form. Frank Lloyd Wright was a master at it. His Unity Temple is one of his first mature expressions of dynamic balance in the Modern sense. Seen from the corner of its site, the building is a contradiction of its name: *Two* masses are visible. The two parts are different, one being the church proper and the other the parish hall. But the two halls are similar enough in construction and configuration to seem both symmetrical and asymmetrical with regard to the entrance axis running between them. In this way, Wright makes a statement about identity, about real differences and false differences, and about the relative values of difference and similarity. This architectural statement is made in the context of a Unitarian church, inviting consideration of the two circumstances of congregation: the religious and the social. Dynamic balance, then, like disjuncture, involves the coordination of independent systems without forcing them into a strict hierarchical order.

A third aspect of the assembly of forms is the *definition of parts through the clear articulation of systems.* This has been an esthetic ideal throughout history and is presumed by disjuncture and dynamic balance. What is particular to the twentieth century is the incorporation of the parts into several systems of building elements. This identification of an element with an independent system acknowledges the nature of standardized production, which is the essence of style, according to both Wright and Le Corbusier. The many different types of glazing in the Villa Savoie—ribbon windows, large glass panes, vertical lights bending around at the base, horizontal lights sliced by the ramp—are organized into an identifiable system by the detailing of the frames (thin, painted steel sections) and by the particular way in which they are joined, consistent within the vocabulary of the window systems but not especially related to any other part of the building. Furthermore, the articulation of the window system is not predictable with regard to the openings in the facades. Sometimes the windows are contained by the openings, but sometimes they are freely disposed. The aim of this

sort of detailing is to allow the glass system to maintain its independence as it interrelates with the wall and structural systems.

In analyzing the formal aspect of the Vitruvian system, it has become clear that many of the characteristics most often attributed to twentieth-century architecture can also be found in earlier styles. But a more precise study has revealed five qualities that seem to pertain particularly to Modern architecture: *integrity of the surfaces and edges of underlying masses, generation of a series of spatial cells from a system of perpendicular transparent planes, disjuncture of formal systems, dynamic balance,* and *the definition of parts through clear articulation of systems.* Certain underlying themes common to these five seem to indicate that a more concise theory is possible. This will be attempted later.

Function

Although the issues in the formal approach to architectural analysis are on the whole straightforward, matters of function have historically been difficult to clarify. It is necessary to begin with a careful definition of the values upon which a functional analysis will be based. Three possible approaches can readily be distinguished: function as use, as purpose, or as structure. The third really has to do with the application of Rationalist principles to the technical side of architecture and will be dealt with later.

In an evaluation based on function as use, the work of architecture is judged by how well it supports the human activities that take place in it. Two standards of judgment have typically been applied to twentieth-century architecture: responsiveness and flexibility. *Responsiveness* refers to the precision with which a building has been tailored to meet its particular functional program. Although it naturally includes an appraisal of how any designated space supports its assigned activities, the standard of responsiveness had been most often applied to circulation areas. In fact, one of the most important generators of the diversity of forms in the twentieth century has been the great amount of attention paid to problems of circulation. Interest in circulation can be traced back at least to the École des Beaux-Arts of the nineteenth century in Paris. Beaux-Arts design is based on solving the circulation of an architectural problem in an initial sketch, the *esquisse,* from which the entire formal design must stem. The characteristic axial system of composition was valued for its clarity of circulation and efficient disposition of functional elements.

The other standard of evaluation for function as use is *flexibility.* This can be interpreted as being opposite to responsiveness if flexibility means accommodating a particular space to a variety of different functions. But it can also be seen as corresponding to responsiveness as a standard by which, for example, a space may continue to support an activity under differing circumstances of daylighting, capacity, and so forth. Here it is interesting to consider how the Beaux-Arts architects valued the Classical orders for their flexibility in application to a wide variety of building types.

This example recalls the second functional approach: *purpose,* a broader-scope view with relevance for iconography in connection with architectural content. It means that the building should represent or express its role in society. An auditorium should present itself as a gathering place, a factory as a workplace, a hospital as a refuge, and so forth. Before the great demographic and social changes of the nineteenth century, the range of functional

possibilities was limited and organized into a rather clear and generally accepted hierarchy. The church and the palace were the two functional prototypes on which architects based other important buildings. It is very significant that the most frequently used models were the largest and grandest examples of church and palace: St. Peter's in Rome, Versailles, and so on. But the twentieth century saw the development of a great many new functional types that did not fit firmly into hierarchical organization. A loss of certainty about cultural values made Classical prototypes untenable and new sources for a code of architectural meaning were sought. In spite of the enormous efforts of architects to base a code upon factories and other industrial buildings, the types that have experienced the greatest development are the private dwelling and the office building. The functional models here are actually small: the minimal standard dwelling unit and working unit.

As has already been mentioned, the styles that Wright and Le Corbusier experimented with seem to depend mostly on iconographic images rather than on a clear distinction between functional types. This is generally true of twentieth-century architecture and is one source of the great diversity of styles so characteristic of this century. An important exception is Alvar Aalto. During his career he managed to conceive and develop distinct prototypes for auditoriums, libraries, churches, office buildings, and apartment houses. His architecture depends most strongly on the interrelation of a clear functional prototype with a direct response to a particular site and environment. Thus, he was one of the first architects to create prototypes on an objective reading of functional requirements rather than from a personal interpretation of the primitive meaning of shelter. It will be shown later that his architecture marks a significant advance in the progress of Modernism in the sense just mentioned and in its confirmation of the unity behind the Wrightian and Corbusian approaches.

A realistic and practical standard for evaluating architecture from the standpoint of function, then, can incorporate function as use—both *flexibility* and *responsiveness*—and function as *purpose*. Some further implications of this will be discussed under the section on iconography.

Technology

One of the justifications heard most frequently from those who supported a new "look" for modern buildings was the fact of technological change. Of course, the changes in construction methods and materials brought about by industrialization had begun long before the appearance of buildings was questioned in this way. In fact, most of the eclectic/revivalist architects of the nineteenth century were ingenious in using the new techniques to produce their Classical and Gothic details. To this day, correctly detailed Greek columns made from fiberglass are readily available as catalog items. It should be recognized, then, that what the proto-Modern architects of the early twentieth century were most strongly reacting against was the meaning that they felt was associated with contemporary references to Classical civilizations. They used the notion of a technological revolution to support their cause.

Tied in with this was the Rationalist point of view. The nineteenth century brought new techniques for determining the configuration of supports necessary for the loads of a building. Some Rationalist critics, asserting that beauty depends on a coherent representation of ultimate truth through reason, took the position that the structural arrangement of a building should be a direct physical analog of the mathematical analysis of loads and forces. Such a position, although attractive, ignores the real nature of modern technology. First, engineering calculations in practice are greatly simplified models of actual conditions. Second, modern construction systems are composite in nature, depending upon the characteristics of more than one material, which introduces complexity into the supposedly straightforward determination of loads and support. Third, construction practices are often more important determinants of building economics than advanced structural theories are. Thus, as far as technological influence is concerned, the Rationalist point of view depends more on the mythicizing of Truth as Beauty and Beauty as Truth than on a truly empirical determination of functional needs through Reason. What is finally important is that the proto-Modern architects felt a need to express some of the forces of technological change within their buildings. They saw these forces as more meaningful to their culture than an assertion of its continuity with a distant Classical past. The expression of technology could be interpreted in any of three ways: through structure, construction, or mechanical systems.

The expression of *structure* has historically been of prime importance in the development of architectural styles. For example, a Classical expression of structure shows the resolution of the great weight of masonry masses by a clearly articulated hierarchy of structural parts. Very different is the expression characteristic of Gothic and Islamic architecture, which is about weightlessness, light-filled vaults, and sparkling, fragmented decorative elements.

Such traditional manifestations became problematic with the development of new structural techniques in the nineteenth century. Gradually, the masonry load-bearing wall with its long history of traditional articulation was transformed into a decorative enclosing screen supported by a steel framework hidden within the building. This in no way interfered with the archeologically correct detailing of the eclectic/revivalist styles, but the hidden presence of the steel framework was disturbing to some architectural critics, who quite reasonably began to speculate on an architecture based on the expression of this frame.

Along with the increase in steel production came the growth of mass-produced plate glass. Precision demands that glass and steel be considered together as a system; furthermore, exposed steel is very susceptible to damage from fire and needs some sort of masonry covering for protection. Therefore, the architects of the Chicago school in the late nineteenth century had in hand a radically new structural system whose appearance then was virtually the same as the older masonry wall-bearing system. The extension of Classical detailing to this situation seems to have been quite natural, a reasonable straightforward expression of the structural frame.

The other important structural system was reinforced concrete, developed mostly in France in the late nineteenth century. Again, the strength of the system lies in its combination of tensile steel reinforcing rods imbedded within concrete members. The expression of such a frame was not very different from that of a fireproofed steel frame, which, as we have seen, resembled older technologies. If the building systems are considered as totalities, then, it is hard to identify a need to overthrow eclectic/revivalist styles on the basis of new structural techniques. But what had in fact changed irrevocably was the scale of major buildings. The standard building types would no longer be the church and palace but the office building and the private home. As long as houses could be the size of palaces and public buildings could approximate Classical models, the Greek and Roman orders could be successfully applied. But when huge skyscrapers, on the one hand, and small dwellings, on the other, became the objects of serious attention, the scaling up or down of correct Classical detailing became problematic.

Le Corbusier's adoption of the Dom-Ino system in his early work left him with an esthetic problem: He wished to express both the lightness of volume and the supporting role of post-and-beam structure. Without the resolution of a clearly supported weight, the columns could become spindly and meaningless. In his later career he designed structures that appeared much more massive, producing a more satisfactory, if Classically derived, reading of load and support.

Frank Lloyd Wright used the contrast between heavy earth-bound masses and apparently floating roofs for expressive purposes. His structural archetypes, the cave and the wigwam or tent, provided a versatile dichotomy for expressing the deep feelings he had for the functions of dwelling and shelter. Such major works as the Johnson Wax Headquarters derive their most profound meaning from the overt interplay of the two archetypes.

There have been many important changes in structural technology that have never been expressed, perhaps because they cannot be expressed. An outstanding example is the development of foundations. Building any type of tall building on Chicago's marshy soil required totally new types of foundations, resulting in the caisson and driven-pile techniques. The only visible evidence for this is that Chicago's buildings, for a while at least, tended to be shorter and broader than those built on Manhattan's bedrock. However, this may just as easily have been the result of the availability of large parcels of property in Chicago right after the great fire of 1871. Certainly, the newest of Chicago's skyscrapers have the same tall, slender profile as those of New York.

In the end, it has to be admitted that the expression of structure is far from just an honest and objective revelation of structural elements. The appearance of any building, as far as expression allows, is a very personal selection on the part of the designer. The famous glass-and-steel buildings of Ludwig Mies van der Rohe rarely show any actual supporting steel. Even where steel is exposed, as at the Illinois Institute of Technology buildings, it is usually some sort of cover plate over the actual supporting element, which is imbedded in protective fireproofing. In this sense, such a use of steel is no more "honest" a representation than aluminum or bronze casings would be, and how far is it from this situation to an applied marble column? Representation of structure need not be identified with the representation of an I-beam.

Just here, a distinction has been made between the expression of structure and the expression of *construction*. How the loads of a building are supported may have only slight association with how that building was made. This is particularly true in the case of poured-in-place concrete. Le Corbusier expresses the means of construction in the Unité d'Habitation at Marseilles by retaining the surface impression left by the wooden forms into which the liquid concrete was poured, thus creating an articulation of surface that contradicts the basic distinction of support (pier) and supported (building block). The apartment block can be read as having been raised above the ground somehow and then propped up by massive piers. But it can also be read as one with the piers, implying that it is a complex plastic form that has been molded into shape or carved out of a solid mass. This reading is suggested by the sculpted shape of the piers and by the even surface rendering left by the form boards. Precast concrete, on the other hand, is usually fabricated

in a manner that relates directly to the support of the building. The ubiquitous precast parking garage is often detailed so that the only expression is the articulation of structural elements.

The new construction systems of the nineteenth century—steel-and-glass and reinforced concrete— encouraged a large-scale plasticity that had been achieved in the past only with great effort, in the vaults and domes of important buildings. In the twentieth century, aside from the curved shells and canopies of specialized single-story structures, this plasticity has most often appeared in the long, unsupported spans and cantilevers of Modern architecture. The prefabrication of structural elements along with the mechanization of construction practices lends itself to an expression of lightness, to volume rather than to the heavy massiveness of Classical architecture. This new expression requires a new attitude toward glass. Glass has been promoted to be a structural material in its own right and can be seen in proto-Modern buildings as a major building element. It is probably the most subtle of all construction materials: The reading of an installation of glass can completely reverse itself from transparent to opaque, from dark to light, depending on the relation between outside and inside lighting conditions. To this extent, glass, like steel and reinforced concrete, also contributes to the new plasticity of twentieth-century architecture.

Glass, steel, and concrete are all processed materials: They are homogeneous and can be manufactured in a variety of shapes, colors, and textures. This is very different from the older materials, such as stone, brick, and wood, all of which have particular characteristics that must be respected in design. But in this century even these have been developed into forms that are more workable. Plywood, bentwood, particle board, veneers, terrazzo, terra-cotta tile, masonry block, and glazed brick are examples of industrialized products made from wood, stone, and brick, all of them homogeneous in nature and available in ranges of shapes, colors, and textures. From such universal control of materials comes the expressive possibilities in modern construction.

A third type of technical expression has developed more recently: the expression of *mechanical systems*. The necessity for providing totally conditioned environments—including ventilation, heating, cooling, power supply, lighting, plumbing, and mechanical conveyance—came from the demands of a developing mass society. Standards of performance were required: It was up to the architect to determine how they were to be met. Responses varied. The architect could ignore these requirements in the design and later provide standard mechanical systems as necessary. Le Corbusier and Wright both used this approach in their limited-budget projects. The architect could incorporate the provisions for environmental conditioning into the formal and structural systems of the building. This was favored by Wright and Le Corbusier when they had the money for it: The heating and ventilating systems of the Johnson Wax Headquarters and the Unité d'Habitation at Marseilles are typical. Or, going even further, the architect could invent entirely new mechanical systems that not only enriched the formal vocabulary of the building but also provided real functional advantages. Wright's radiant floor heating and Le Corbusier's *brise-soleil* are famous examples of this attitude.

For Modern architecture, then, the third Vitruvian element, technology, can be broken down into three modes of expression: structure, construction and mechanical systems. Although in the past Rationalist arguments have been made in support of these, it is clear that the degree to which they are expressed is dependent upon the personal values held by the designer. Those who would argue for a deterministic technology need to acknowledge this.

The three parts of the conventional Vitruvian approach to architectural analysis have now been adapted for the twentieth century. It is clear that a stylistic breakdown could be based, as it has in the past, on the formal element. This would group buildings according to the degree to which they resemble each other, an organization based on surface readings and a certain degree of common sense. The formal element, however, fails to account for the *progress* of architectural style. Particularly in the twentieth century, it is at least as important to explore what makes styles change as it is to define them with precision. Such an exploration would have to focus on the relation between architecture and the larger cultural values from which it derives, the degree to which it reflects its own society as opposed to the universal values of Western civilization. For example, the traditional history of architecture, centered on the Vitruvian element of form, seems to focus on Italian developments and extends itself only with great difficulty to such problematic cultures as the British. It seems that the difference between, say, Palladio and Palladianism cannot be sufficiently accounted for on the level of form alone.

The other two Vitruvian elements, function and technology, do not make up for the gap between form and meaning. Although Rationalism and Functionalism appear to connect architecture with the larger values of society, it has been shown that the ostensible objectivity of these two approaches is more wish than reality. Certainly function and technology must be taken into account in analyzing a work of architecture, but there is no independent standard of value inherent in either.

For the purposes of this study, then, the Vitruvian

criteria have been found limited on two grounds: first, they do not account for the *revolutionary* quality of Modern architecture, for its important differences from all architectures of the past; and second, they tell little about the supposed differences between Frank Lloyd Wright and Le Corbusier. In this sense, of course, it confirms the presumption that the two great architects were not very different after all in their basic approaches to Modernism. But there is still a need to compare their work in a better way. For this, and for isolating the defining characteristics of Modern architecture, there needs to be a fourth element: iconography.

Iconography

In the simplest terms, iconographic analysis is used to identify standards of meaning behind a work of architecture for the inhabitants of its own time and place, whereas formal analysis can be strictly applied to the larger, unchanging esthetic principles that are universal in application. Thus, the iconographic element explores the possibilities of architecture as a medium of communication. As the limitations of Vitruvian analysis have become apparent to theoreticians of twentieth-century architecture, they have attempted to use some of the ideas of modern language theory to establish an iconography for architecture, both modern and of the past. Christian Norberg-Schulz, Robert Venturi, and Manfredo Tafuri have all written important theoretical studies from this point of view and it must be ranked among the more important strands of modern critical theory.

Another aspect of the iconographic element is that it represents the interests of the user personifying the culture at large. This allows for a more just evaluation of an architect's proper responsibility. Instead of blind insistence on accountability for the entire project, four distinct sources of influence can be determined: the architect for the formal design, the owner for functional and economic constraints, the builder for technological considerations, and the user who stands for the society at large.

By taking such an approach, one also becomes aware of the propaganda value of architecture. Buildings through their appearance give identity and value both to the individual and to social institutions. The Gothic cathedral was built as a representation of Heaven itself, the worshipper being identified as one of the Christian community and therefore worthy of salvation. By adopting the architectural motifs and images developed in the cathedrals, the guilds and municipalities of the Middle Ages identified themselves with the Christian corpus in their secular buildings. During the Renaissance, people looked to their Classical past for acknowledgment of the continuity of their civilization. Buildings were based on Roman prototypes without any necessary regard for their ancient functions, for the purpose beneath this was to validate the developing imperial state by demonstrating its continuity with a glorious past. As scholarship began to refine this image, architecture developed iconographically into archeologically correct revivalism and eclecticism. But a continuing expansion of historical knowledge made references to older times more and more ambiguous. Were the Greeks more suitable as models than the Romans? How could an age conceived of as "dark" have produced Chartres, Rheims, and Amiens?

Much of the strange-looking architecture produced between 1890 and 1920 can best be understood if one sees that the forms and images of revivalism were still in use after the meaning behind them had been for all intents and purposes rejected. The development of a Modern architecture depended then on establishing a new basis for meaning. Only empiricism, the belief in an objective and accepting view of the emerging industrialized mass society of the turn of the century, had the power to overturn the deeply rooted faith in Classicism. It is pertinent in this regard that functional types, as has been previously pointed out, switched from the church and palace of Beaux-Arts Classicism to the office building and private home of Wright and Le Corbusier. Behind the celebration of the working individual that motivates Modern architecture and generates its machine imagery is a new consciousness: a willingness to surrender cherished Rationalist beliefs in favor of empirically obtained data, even if that data could not yet be resolved into a tightly organized hierarchy of values such as that espoused by Classicistic civilization.

For an architectural style to become fully developed it must tap some source of collective social expression. The architect's meaning must be stated in terms that can be understood by the owner, the builder, and the user. Wright's early architecture was supported by middle-class businessmen in suburban Oak Park, Illinois. His message at that time was about the nature of the family and its shelter. Consequently, he was popular as a residential architect, but not as a downtown business architect. His one major office building, the Larkin, was given to him by Darwin Martin, who liked Wright's houses. In its celebration of the working environment it was advanced for its day and had no successors until the Johnson Wax Headquarters thirty years later. By then, progressive socialism had become respectable in comparison with more radical political movements of the thirties. Again in the 1950s, Wright's Price Tower in Bartlesville, Oklahoma displayed a mixture of living and working accommodation that was not fully accepted until certain mixed-use skyscrapers of the 1970s.

For Le Corbusier, success came in the 1920s when his Maison Dom-Ino system, intended for mass-produced workers' housing, was adapted for luxury town houses and villas by the more radical intellectuals of Paris. His League of Nations competition entry, courageously expressing the equivalence of the Congress Hall, seating the delegates, and the Secretariat, housing the support staff, was rejected in favor of a centralized, hierarchical scheme that subordinated the worker's offices to the ceremonial meeting hall. His own scheme for a multiuse skyscraper was finally constructed at Marseilles (the Unité d'Habitation) at the intervention of a particularly progressive official of the French government.

Architecture as propaganda depends upon a working knowledge of the languages and "dialects" inherent in architectural images. This was understood by the eclectic/revivalist architects of the nineteenth century. Because they wished to express contemporary society's connection with ancient civilizations, they felt free to select images from past styles and to use them in contemporary contexts. In the same vein, the early Modern architects had to abandon those images. What they came up with instead was based upon industrial buildings and vernacular housing, which were both more appropriate for the new buildings types—office building and private dwelling—and had propagandistic appeal in the growing labor democracies of the West.

Manfredo Tafuri[43] writes of a collaboration between architect and critic, both sharing the continuing effort to develop relevant styles and often exchanging roles. The critic interprets architectural projects, indicating the meanings associated with the forms, and attempts to create a verbal parallel to the esthetic position established within the architecture. In this sense, the criticial process is descriptive. On the other hand, the architect's role is generative to the degree that the work supplements or enriches the language of architecture. A generative grammar has long been the goal of verbal linguists and an experiment was made by Christian Norberg-Schulz in his *Intentions in Architecture* to develop a generative and critical grammar for architecture. In this sense, the critic can be a partner with the architect in the development of a meaningful architectural language.

At the core of the critical situation is the question: What is the content of Modern architecture? At least two levels of content can be identified. The first may be termed the *prosaic* level. It is intellectual, matter-of-fact, and dependent upon logic and reason. It is the level more easily written about and objectively evaluated. It is also more easily grasped in commonsense terms.

Within the prosaic level, two sublevels of communication can be identified: the functional and the purposive. *Functional* communication has to do with the building's ability to inform the user about its use. Is the entrance clearly marked? Can one find one's way around? Does the ambience of a particular area support the activity it was meant to house? *Purposive* communication calls mostly upon the cognitive functions of memory and consideration and depends less upon direct perception. Does the building resemble others of its type? Are its parts articulated in such a way that the intent of the builders can be ascertained? What value does the building claim for its ostensible purpose? Much of the potential for architectural communication comes from the interplay of the actual functional configuration with the iconographic functional communication. The configuration of a hall or auditorium, for example, can equally suit a theater, a church, or a mortuary. It is through the presentation of this configuration to the user that appropriate relative values can be communicated.

The second level of content—the *poetic*—has in recent years been the subject of much critical discussion. The wholesale application of the International Style after World War II to the building programs of an expanding society was attempted without a sympathetic understanding of all of its implications. Tenets of the International Style, such as "form follows function" and "less is more," became catchphrases for a merely prosaic involvement with the problematic philosophies of Rationalism and Functionalism, taken much too literally. The result was a great silence at the deeper poetic level, a profound emptiness that architects attempted to fill with melodramatic, romanticized versions of form, function, and technology. Form was romanticized as "pure form," a Platonic mystification of simple geometric shapes outside any realistic context. Function was romanticized with abrupt, angular gestures in plan, section, and elevation, which were explained as "responses" or "inflections" to circumstances of program and environment. Technology was romanticized through the use of elaborate and overstated structural and mechnical systems. And all of this was no more than the inflation of the prosaic level of meaning to hide the essential emptiness beneath. Buildings with these romantic qualities have been repeatedly described as "abstract" and "cold," terms that indicate communication between building and user was incomplete. More recently, the prosaic level of iconographic content itself has been romanticized in elaborate schemes of Classical revival and eclecticism, which ignore the limitations within which an individual of the Modern world may regard cultural history.

So, critical theory today has as its main concern the salvation of the poetic, an effort that requires a clear and comprehensive review of the principles and beliefs that determined the architecture known as *Modern*. For the purposes of this study, two areas of concern at the poetic level will be explored: response to shelter and response to environment.

Response to shelter involves the individual's relation to the natural world. Both Wright and Le Corbusier displayed consciousness of this issue in their exaggerated prototypical images of shelter (fig. 5-1). Wright's Prairie style hip roofs, his later cantilevered roof planes, and his wigwam or tent structural archetype are examples of shelter imagery. Likewise, Le Corbusier expressed shelter in his vaulted roofs and later in his freestanding parasols. Both he and Wright used cave and tent imagery in profound recognition not just of functional and technological ideas but of the poetic potential of such archetypes.

Response to environment is about the individual's role within social units. In addition to shelter images, Wright and Le Corbusier also used prototypical *cloister* images that deal with the separation of particular groups of individuals from society at large for a shared purpose (fig. 5-1). The sky-caves of Wright's Larkin and Johnson buildings, Guggenheim Museum, and Annie Pfeiffer Chapel, as well as Le Corbusier's Senate Chamber at Chandigarh and monastery chapel at La Tourette, are examples of cloisters that offer protection from society for the contemplative individual just as the shelter protects the active individual from nature.

The poetic level of content deals finally with faith and belief. It might be said that the architects of the late nineteenth century were faced with the exhaustion of cultural values. The two major stylistic tracks—the Picturesque and Beaux-Arts Classicism—had lost the conviction of their predecessors, the Gothic and Greek revivals. As the industrialization of the Western world proceeded, it became less and less realistic to hold on either to medievalist

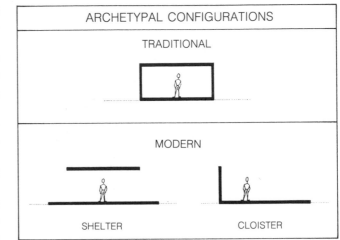

5-1. Functional prototypes in Modern architecture.

romanticism on the one hand or to Platonic idealism on the other. Thus, the Picturesque, which stemmed from a celebration of natural incident and circumstance, developed into estheticism and Art Nouveau, based on the extremes of sensation and the subconscious. This truly Expressionistic strain remains parallel to but separate from mainstream Modernism throughout the twentieth century.

It is rather with the other, the Rationalist strain, that Wright and Le Corbusier achieved a major transformation. The classical belief in a unified, hierarchical order—no longer tenable in the multifarious and dynamic civilization of the industrial age—had to be abandoned in favor of a more legitimate expression of a disjointed but coordinated collision of belief systems. The manifestation of this pioneering transformation in architecture can be shown through direct comparison of Wright's early work with Le Corbusier's.

6 Wright and Le Corbusier as Pioneers:
Early Work in Comparison

The trailblazing characteristics of Wright's and Le Corbusier's work become apparent when the modified Vitruvian approach, derived in the preceding chapter, is used in comparing their work.

Form

The first characteristic of form is *the expression of mass through the integrity of edges and surfaces.* In Wright's Isabel Roberts House of 1908 he employs his typical *parti* of a low element intersecting a higher element, forming a cross in plan (fig. 6-1). The elements themselves demonstrate a clearly stratified opposition of masonry (stucco in the original, now replaced by brick), wood-and-glass ribbon window, and flat hip roof. The masonry consists of simply rendered slabs and piers that are taller and denser near the central intersection, marked by the tallest slab of all at the chimney, and lower at the extremes of the wings, except for isolated piers supporting the porch roof at the southern end. The horizontal edges of the slabs have (or originally had) wide bands of wooden trim, stained dark. These bands can become part of the ribbon window system, as

does the roof-edge trim, depending on the alignment of the band of windows. The insistent horizontal thrust of the masses is emphasized by this trim, which, used consistently as an edge, regulates the joining of the three systems. Dynamically, the tall wing seems to have pushed itself through the lower wing, plowing fragments of it forward to become a planter at the foot. The reading is similar inside, where light entering from the right and left of the central fireplace beneath the balcony implies the extension of space crosswise through the main living room. The cohesiveness of the house is achieved by the total support that each element, each detail gives to the overall *parti*. All is handled with the simplest expression of edge and surface.

A very similar coherency can be seen in Le Corbusier's Maisons La Roche-Jeanneret of 1924 (fig. 6-1b). The original project of 1922 showed a long, simply expressed block connected by a bridge to a smaller slab in the garden. In the final work as executed, a much more subtle interconnection of the masses was achieved. The main block was given a projecting element at the street end, which corresponds to a recessed element at the garden

6-1a. Wright: Isabel Roberts House, River Forest, Illinois, 1908.

6-1b. Le Corbusier: Maisons La Roche-Jeanneret, Paris, 1924.

corner. This recessed element is detailed so that it seems to pass under the curved block, now lifted on *pilotis*. Subtle differences in the treatment of the large glass window on each of these minor blocks make it appear that the connecting block has been pushed back and squeezed between the two main blocks and that the projecting element has popped out in response. All this is reinforced by the entry hall within the recessed block from which the space punctures the walls of the blocks on either side, and through which bridgelike passages float. As in the Wright house, there is a dynamic push of one space through another expressed through simple surfaces and a careful definition of edge conditions.

The second formal characteristic of twentieth-century architecture has been identified as *generation of a system of spatial cells by transparent planes perpendicular to each other*. Wright, in his early work, developed a plaid of spaces squeezed or stretched between masonry masses. Alignment of the masses is determined by transparent planes. In the Darwin Martin House of 1904, these defining planes can be clearly made out on the plan (fig. 6-2a). From the outside, the simple masonry piers are organized into corresponding pairs that strongly imply interpenetrating planes through the emphasized continuity of surface and through the expression of structural bearing. Inside, the continuity of these brick piers is maintained and the generating planes can be read from their surfaces and from the variation of light and dark, which helps to layer the space in parallel strips. This reading is supported by the wood strips at the edges of the low cornice just below the ceilings. These strips define the planes that generate the brick piers and outline the perimeters of the various rooms.

For Le Corbusier, the planar generating system took on the form of a Cartesian grid in plan. The

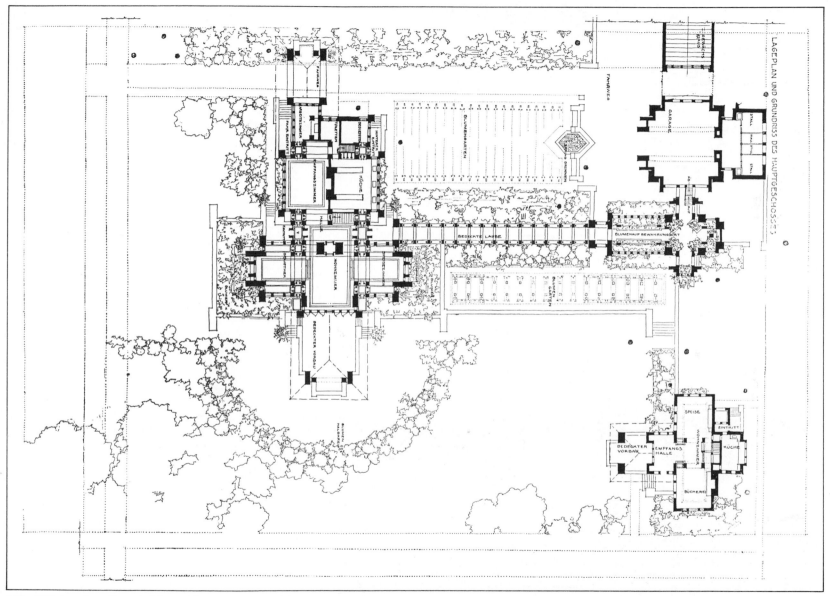

6-2a. Wright: plan, Darwin Martin House, Buffalo, 1904.

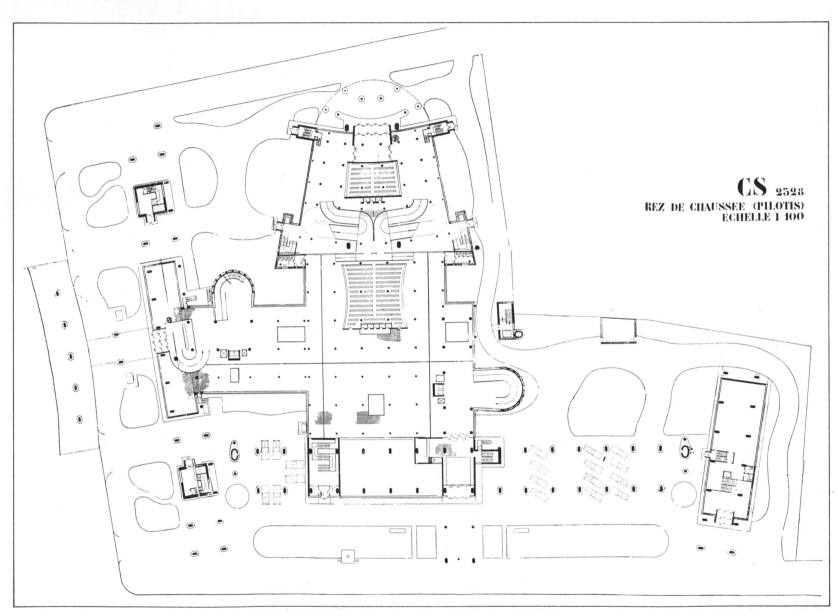

CS 2528
REZ DE CHAUSSÉE (PILOTIS)
ECHELLE 1 100

6-2b. Le Corbusier: plan, Palais du Centrosoyus, Moscow, 1929. (Courtesy of Fondation Le Corbusier.)

development of the design from a straightforward orthogonal grid to a subtle composite of variations can be seen in his project for the Palais du Centrosoyus in Moscow, designed in 1928–29 and finnally executed without supervision in the middle 1930s (fig. 6-2b). In the final version, different exigencies of circulation are allowed to affect the grid so that the two main entries, for example, penetrate a double row of piers stretched both in their own section and toward the direction of passage. The hall beyond is a straightforward regular grid of columns that becomes, below the main auditorium, slightly bent according to the curved rows of seating above. Nodes in the circulation are strongly curved against the grid, which is expressed in plan and elevation as hairline joints between rectilinear building elements. By minimizing surface distinctions between the different building materials and by subtly expressing different jointing patterns, Le Corbusier used the traces of the planar grid as the major articulating system for the building.

The third aspect of twentieth-century form is *disjuncture*. The "exploded" quality that has been so often commented upon with regard to Wright's Robie House of 1906 comes from his maintaining a visual separation between the roof, wall, and window systems (fig. 6-3a). Unlike many of his cruciform houses, the solid masonry core is reversed here so that the central portion lifts above its base and is anchored by masses at the ends beneath the porches. The house is a composite, inside and out, of the three main systems, which intersect to form a Modern space.

Le Corbusier's expression of disjuncture has been previously discussed in relation to the Villa Savoie (fig. 6-3b). Here, as at the Robie House, none of the four systems—*pilotis,* screen walls, windows, or circulation core—is dominant. The windows can be

6-3a. Wright: Robie House.

simply infill between screen walls, as is the large glass light between the living room and terrace, or actual punctures through the wall, as on the facade. They might follow the line of *pilotis,* as on two facades, or slide past them, as on the other two. The house has the composite quality of a collage.

The quality of *dynamic balance* is very subtly treated by the two masters. Wright's Hardy House of 1905 appears to have the symmetry and repose of a classical temple (figs. 6-4a and 6-5a). Beautifully proportioned, its static presence is not at all like the thrusting restlessness of the cruciform Prairie houses. The limits of its own cross-shaped plan are carefully controlled by the simple rectilinear roof plane, a typical Wright molding at its edge. But in approaching and entering the house, different forces are brought

6-3b. Le Corbusier: Villa Savoie.

into play. The approach must be made sharply from either side, at an angle from which the house appears to be breaking through its street-side wall. The off-center chimney responds to the terracing of the house down the steep slope at the rear of the site. Although the strict symmetry of the house on the street elevation suggests an axial entrance, the axis as a physical manifestation has been "erased" from the elevation. No sharp line or central feature marks the center of symmetry, and entry must be made through one of two widely separated but identical doors. It is clear from the plan that there is no functional reason for this split entry; Wright easily could have worked in a central door. What the Hardy House represents, then, is Wright's attempt to establish a dynamic balance between circulation as function and form. It is a formally symmetrical plan that must be used asymmetrically.

This superimposition of symmetrical and asymmetrical systems was used in a very similar way by Le Corbusier in the Villa Stein at Garches of 1927 (figs. 6-4b and 6-5b). Again, three wide bays in plan are separated by two narrow circulation bays. Again, a wall is penetrated on the approach side and the house opens to terraces on the garden side. Of course, the twin entrances are differentiated at Garches; there is a major and a minor door. But the same stretching of the facade and insistence on an off-axis approach results in an "erasing" of the centerline. Again, there is a dynamic balance between function and form.

The final characteristic of Modern form is *the definition of parts through clear articulation.* The differentiation of the two main halls at Wright's Unity Temple of 1904 has already been remarked upon (fig. 6-6a). The stair towers of the church are clearly marked on the outside as independent blocks standing in the corners of the cruciform room. Vertical

6-4a. Wright: Hardy House, Racine, 1905.

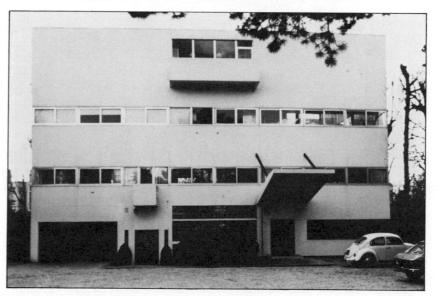

6-4b. Le Corbusier: Villa Stein, Garches, 1927.

Wright and Le Corbusier as Pioneers 95

6-5a. Wright: Hardy House.

6-5b. Le Corbusier: Villa Stein.

walls are decisively stopped at their tops by horizontal bands that cast dark shadow lines. Vertical reveals do the same for differing functional masses. Inside, the space is more ambiguous. The large-scale structural elements so prominent on the outside become mysterious forms behind the tracery screens covering the surfaces of the walls and balconies. But the order of the parts, their organization into systems, remains clear.

Le Corbusier's Maison Planex of 1927 exhibits a similar consciousness in the articulation of its parts (fig. 6-6b). Cruciform in plan, the central thrust of the second-floor bedroom through the plane of the street facade is expressed at the joint by a change in window detail. The top of the skylight can be seen behind the facade, implying the further penetration of the crosswing beyond into the garden. Doors, windows, structural columns, and circulation elements are all differentiated by clean joints where they intersect and by revealed details appropriate to the construction of each.

Function

A functional analysis of twentieth-century architecture, as has been pointed out, must make distinctions between function as *use* and function as *purpose*. The former can be further broken down into two aspects: *responsiveness* and *flexibility*. The responsiveness of Frank Lloyd Wright's Robie House to domestic activity is heightened by its restricted site. The inability of Wright to extend the house laterally as a composite of functionally separate pavilions— his favorite *parti*—forced him to stratify the functions vertically. Recreational family activities are left at ground level and protected from the sidewalk by a narrow courtyard. The main entertainment level is the second floor, consisting of living room, dining room, and study. Bedrooms occur on the third level. Service at each level comes from a smaller pavilion, attached at a corner, that has a garage at ground level, kitchen adjacent to the dining room on the second floor, and bedrooms on the third floor. The association of recreational functions is recognized in the connections between the four rooms on the first and second floors. The open fireplace and stair-well between the living and dining rooms, in fact, link the two functional areas on either end of a single pavilionlike floor. The original furniture, specially built for the house, supported a close connection between detailing and function, contributing to an impression of overall coherence.

Le Corbusier's first scheme for the Villa Savoie had servant spaces on the ground floor, main living spaces on the second floor, and a private bedroom suite on the third level, overlooking the terrace. The bedrooms were on the approach side and the main living rooms faced the garden at the back, an arrangement totally different from Wright's typical plans. In the final scheme, as built, the third bedroom is moved from the roof down to the second floor and the other rooms are reduced in size to accommodate it. A roof terrace remains as a vestige of this suite. Circulation is forced through the living spaces, somewhat like in the Robie House, although Wright's more typical approach was to thread circulation across the ends of functional spaces. The rooms' informal, asymmetrical configuration could accept only the most casual arrangement of furniture, acknowledgment of the use of the house as a country retreat.

Flexibility of use was a determinant of the configuration of Wright's Midway Gardens of 1914. An enclosed restaurant block with underground kitchen could operate independently in the winter and in conjunction with a large outdoor garden in the summer. Because much of the seating was placed on

6-6a. Wright: Unity Temple, Oak Park, 1904.

6-6b. Le Corbusier: Maison Planex, Paris, 1927.

balconies or mezzanines both inside and outside, a greatly varying number of patrons could be accommodated, depending on the season. The restaurants would nearly always seem occupied, if not full, and service could be concentrated according to the capacity.

In his Cité du Réfuge for the Salvation Army, Le Corbusier provided a clear distinction between the public meeting functions in front and the private residential slab behind. At the main level, one story above grade, a dining area united both public and private functions. The bedrooms above could be left as open dormitories or as nurseries, or they could be converted into private rooms. The roof levels had small individual rooms with terraces for mothers and babies. Men and women could be separated by floor or on any given floor, two dormitories could be made totally exclusive of each other on either side of the main stair. The provision for flexibility of accommodation without losing the scale of the whole was very similar to that found in the Midway Gardens.

Wright's Larkin Building of 1903 is a prime example of how the functional level of purpose can be handled along with responsiveness and flexibility. For Wright, working meant concentrating on a task and his workplaces were designed to support concentration. The Larkin Building allowed no direct views to the surroundings but permitted daylight to enter through clerestory windows and skylights. Except for the executives housed in an adjacent slab, the entire staff occupied one huge room together, with tiers of galleries dedicated to the different activities of the working day. Offices, open work tables, a cafeteria, and recreation rooms were all accommodated. The exterior was expressed as simple masonry service blocks at the corners, bridged by windowed terraces. Detailing was straightforward and large in scale, expressive of a no-nonsense attitude toward communal labor.

It was the celebration of communal labor, perhaps, that defeated Le Corbusier's entry for the Palace of the League of Nations Competition of 1927–28. As a freestanding element, his Secretariat was given equal prominence to the Congress Hall block. The equivalency of function thus expressed, with its clear-headed recognition of the bureaucratic nature of international diplomacy, was anathema to the competition jury, which premiated a Beaux-Arts design that celebrated the Congress Hall as the central feature.

Technology

As has been proposed in the preceding chapter, the technological aspects of modern architecture can be considered in three ways: *structure, construction*, and *mechanical systems*. Frank Lloyd Wright viewed structure as a stark representation of supporting versus supported. The hip roofs of the Darwin Martin House seem to float between isolated masonry piers, with the rows of windows slung beneath. The extension of space from inside to outside is correlated to sweeping cantilevers at the eaves. The heavy masonry platforms and piers that support the house are fractured by the pressure of the space within.

Le Corbusier approached structure from a completely different point of view. For him, the lightness and regularity of an exposed skeletal frame expressed a sophisticated logical clarity quite different from the drama of Wrightian cantilevers. At the Maison Cook of 1926, the thinnest possible concrete columns support floor slabs framed with shallow beams. The thinness of the facade adds to the impression of lightness. The same is true of the post-supported roof of the top-story garden. The columns and screen walls spring directly from the ground, with no indication of foundations.

Wright's attitude toward construction can be identified in Unity Temple. The walls are poured-in-place reinforced concrete, one of the earliest uses of this material left exposed. A special pebble aggregate was placed against the form and revealed by hosing down the still-wet concrete after the form boards were stripped. Interior finishes consist mostly of painted concrete or plaster over concrete. Elaborate screen moldings are fashioned from simple pieces of milled finish lumber. Stained glass windows have a repeated, rectilinear pattern. All of this is geared toward site-finished or specially adapted mass-produced materials. Assembly required skilled laborers, if not craftsmen, able enough to understand a unique application of a particular material.

Le Corbusier's Cité du Réfuge for the Salvation Army was meant to be assembled from parts that, if not yet standardized, at least resembled the basic elements that would be fabricated as standard for buildings of the machine age. The poured concrete frame is finished smooth and the stuccoed walls painted either white or a deep color. A factory-glazed tile is used for important wall surfaces along the entrance. Large lights of glass with the simplest of metal frames were originally installed, later to be supplemented with a *brise-soleil*. And where Wright would have had a custom-patterned stained glass, Le Corbusier uses an elegantly detailed but standardized glass block. Although the building as a prototype required a great deal of custom finishing, the components were all designed to look as if they could be used anywhere. The building expresses the independence of factory mass-produced parts.

Wright's treatment of mechanical systems was to work them into the structural fabric of his buildings.

In the Robie House the radiators and pipes are hidden beneath the floor or behind panels below the windowsills. Lighting is either exposed in a custom-fabricated fixture or recessed into the ceiling behind wooden grilles. This suppression of the actual devices that produce the heat or light is very much in keeping with his control of natural daylight and sunlight. Spaces above the ceilings of his houses were used for a sophisticated system of natural ventilation coordinated with the casement windows. The eaves kept direct sun from entering the rooms in summer, but allowed diffused light to reflect inside from their light-painted soffits. For Wright, the fact of mechanical supplementation of light and heat was unimportant and incidental to the experience of the building. The device that he did choose to celebrate was the fireplace. In the Robie House this element stands free between the living room and dining room, a sculptural and structural element as well as a source of heat. Water in a recessed pool around the hearth would reflect the image of the flames.

The mechanical systems of Le Corbusier's Villa Savoie are similar to those of the Robie House in configuration. The radiators of the living/dining room are exposed below the built-out sill of the ribbon windows. Indirect lighting is available from an exposed fixture hanging below the ceiling. Full-height glass doors open to a terrace, but instead of the row of modular openings of the Robie House, the Villa Savoie has a sliding glass light operated with a crank. Finally, the freestanding fireplace is neither large nor prominently placed. It is simply built, its flue no great sculptured stack but merely a pipe leading up to the ceiling. It is an appurtenance, circumstantial in nature and dispensable in practice. Its appearance seems to have been decided not by the designer of the house but by the manufacturer.

6-7a. Wright: Baker House. Wilmette, Illinois, 1909. (From *Frank Lloyd Wright to 1910* by Grant Carpenter Manson. © 1958 by Van Nostrand Reinhold Company, Inc. Reprinted by permission of the publisher.)

Le Corbusier goes further than Wright in expressing the independence of mechanical components.

Iconography

The basis for a comparison between Wright and Le Corbusier must finally rest upon the interpretation of their iconographies. It has been pointed out how historians have traditionally assumed that they stood in opposition to each other. It has also been shown that there are in fact differences between their ideas about the city versus nature and about machine production. But of far greater importance is the revelation of a common language between the two men, a language they understood from observation of the new culture developing around them during their careers. The elements of this language, then, will be explored by comparing a house representative of an ideal dwelling unit in each of their oeuvres:

for Wright, the Baker House (1909), a perfected Prairie type in Wilmette, Illinois; for Le Corbusier, the Atelier Ozenfant (1922), a classic compact studio-house in Paris.

With regard to *functional communication,* the first aspect of the *prosaic* level of iconographic content, it may be said that the Baker House is a distillation, presented analytically, of a typical suburban house of its time and place (fig. 6-7a). It occupies a plot of the same size—about a quarter-acre—as other houses on the street and it addresses the street in the same polite manner, orthogonally. The low, extended roof forms a porte cochere, providing a clear expression of how an automobile is to approach the house. Typical of Wright, the front door is more difficult to find at first, although an interruption by a solid pier in the first-floor row of windows marks its location. The high story-and-a-half windows of the main projecting block define the living room within as the chief occupiable space, and the broad chimney visible above the intersection of the wings marks the solid center. The extension of the first-floor wing beyond the living room block to a second porch completes the demonstration of circulation between the spaces, clearly discernible before the house is even entered. This is achieved with Wright's typical clarity of massing and ordering of shapes, enhanced with the simplest possible rendering of plain, white surfaces and the framing of modular windows in strips of dark wood.

Inside, the great lateral stretch of the house across the site is marked by a single continuous wall incorporating the fireplace at its center (fig. 6-8a). The street side of this wall is for public and family living, whereas the yard side is reserved for private and service rooms. The very subtle way in which the main stair along the wall slides up to the bedrooms and the upstairs balcony protrudes into the living room reinforces the sense of this wall as a screen between the social and individual activities of the family (fig. 6-9a). The openness of the social rooms on the public side of the screen expresses the continuity of social living and accommodates a variety of activities. Continuity with the outdoors is encouraged by the great number of opening windows and doors along the walls, by the two porches, by the three-sided exposure of the living room, and by identical detailing inside and out. Although provision for a small staff was incorporated into the house, the strict hierarchy of social activities enforced by Neoclassical planning is erased here, along with the dividing partitions in the social wings of the house.

Observing Le Corbusier's Atelier Ozenfant, one is struck again by the respect shown for the context of the neighborhood (fig. 6-7b). It stands on its tight little corner shoulder-to-shoulder with the party walls

6-7b. Le Corbusier: Atelier Ozenfant, Paris, 1922.

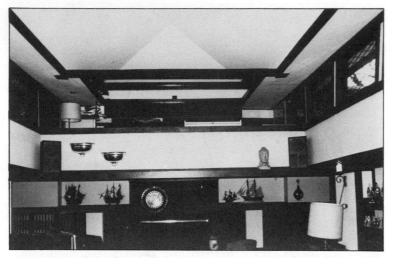

6-8a. Wright: Baker House.

6-8b. Le Corbusier: Atelier Ozenfant. (Courtesy of Fondation Le Corbusier.)

of adjoining houses. A slight projection of the second floor slab shadows both the vehicular and twin pedestrian entrances, similar to the much more extreme roof projections of the Wright house. And where the Wright house defined circulation by a horizontal progression of void to narrow ribbon window to tall window, the Le Corbusier house offers the same progression vertically, from the subtly expressed void at the ground level, past the private rooms on the second floor, to the main living room with its tall story-and-a-half areas of glass. Even the mullion pattern is similar to that of the Baker House, twin verticals above a single vision light. The low parapet that defines the path from the driveway to the front door of the Baker House is twisted vertically into a spiral at the Atelier Ozenfant, surrounding the circular stair to the main entry. Both houses offer more immediate entry into service areas directly from the driveway.

Inside, the Atelier Ozenfant is divided horizontally into public and private areas by the third-floor slab in a manner analogous to the continuous dividing wall of the Baker House. Even the response of vertical circulation is similar, the discontinuity between the vertical stair up to the third floor and subordinate stairs to mezzanines above the studio emphasizing the third floor in the way that the main stair in the Baker House emphasized the dividing wall. The lifting of roof planes above the main living areas is common to both houses, and the continuity of simply rendered materials inside and out is again to be found in the Atelier Ozenfant. The small fireplace in the studio, placed, as in the Baker House, beneath a small mezzanine library, is stressed (fig. 6-8b). The corners are important in their expression of vertical protection and privacy from the rest of the crowded street, and where Le Corbusier emphasizes this at the intersection of the glass walls by leaving

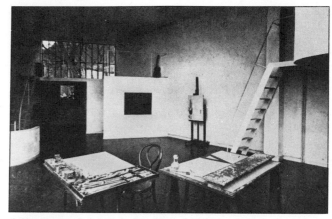

6-9b. Le Corbusier: Atelier Ozenfant. (Courtesy of Fondation Le Corbusier.)

6-9a. Wright: Baker House.

a solid corner post dark against the light pouring in on either side, Wright does everything he can to dematerialize his corners (fig. 6-9b).

To turn to the *purposive* aspect of the prosaic level of iconographic content, the Baker House is revealed as a house by its relation to the street across a lawn, by the protection of its entry, and by its hip roofs. Although its appearance was startling in 1909 because of the lowness, great horizontal extension, and simplicity of detailing, the size and number of its coordinated living pavilions definitely express residential use. The Baker House is an example of a type designed by Wright for a specific group of people new to the American scene: self-made businessmen. The values of these individuals are woven tightly into the Prairie house fabric; when the type was stretched, as in the Coonley House and the McCormick project, a sort of diffused, amorphous uneasiness began to appear in the design. The strict, hierarchical social rites of the aristocracy were accommodated only with difficulty within the flexible, coordinated pavilions of Prairie architecture.

Wright and Le Corbusier as Pioneers 103

In Europe, however, it was the intellectuals and artists of the so-called Bohemian avant-garde who formed a new group important for the development of European culture. There was no natural place for it in the traditional hierarchy of European society. Membership in the group depended not on wealth, family background, or political power, but solely on belief in a particular set of progressive values. The Bohemian world existed parallel to the traditional class system; one could live a Bohemian life and still maintain one's position in a traditional class. The common idea behind the values of the Bohemians, in whatever manifestation they appeared in a particular society, was the denial of centuries-old beliefs, beliefs that had generated traditional society but that could no longer be sincerely held by those sensitive to the prima facie evidence of the rapidly changing world around them. In Europe, it is from this group that most of the great determining ideas for Modern culture derived. Le Corbusier belonged to the Bohemian world and it was for them that he developed his studio-house prototype. The flatly rendered stucco walls and simple glass openings of the Atelier Ozenfant are in the tradition of living-quarters-plus-workshop inhabited by artisans and copied by the artists of Bohemian Paris. Whereas Wright only rarely incorporated a working area into his houses (those for himself being the most striking exceptions), the studio space was basic to Le Corbusier's functional iconography. As the hip roofs of the Baker House symbolize its residential function, the little factory sawtooth skylights originally built above the Atelier Ozenfant expressed both the working environment below and, representationally, the industrial character of its construction.

Thus, at the prosaic level, each architect emphasized directly the values of a newly emergent social group that would lead the procession of Western societies into the modern era. The values that distinguished them were expressed by distilling the characteristics of surrounding houses into a disturbing, analytical statement. At the same time, the adoption by both architects of almost identical techniques of finishing and detailing are symptomatic of their rejection of traditional values expressing the continuity of the ruling classes with great civilizations of the past. The new class—the prosperous upper-middle in America and the Bohemian intellectual in Europe—now defined itself from new values, rejecting, at least for a while, important parts of traditional culture.

This conscious attempt at establishing a new architectural language based on an empirical evaluation of form, function, and technology manifests itself as well at the deeper poetic level of iconographic content. Beginning with the first of the two themes identified earlier, *response to shelter,* the Baker House can be seen to explore the potential of the horizontal. Lightly poised, its floating roofs imply that man's place in nature is secure, needing only minimal reinforcement for protection from discomfort. Interaction with the natural environment is encouraged by large areas of glass, opening doors and windows, and porches. Privacy is maintained by patterns on the glass, rendering it virtually opaque from the outside, although the continuity of the horizontal roof within is expressed by the deep shadow lines below the eaves. The emphasis on the fireplace at the center of the main organizing wall of the house in the living room adds fire to the experience of the other natural elements, earth and air. (Where he could afford it, Wright occasionally introduced the fourth element, water, with a pool surrounding the hearth as in the Robie and Barnsdall houses.) For Wright, then, the essence of modern civilization was a new attitude toward the natural environment, a complete rejection of the fear he believed had generated earlier architectures and, to an extent, the modern city.

At the Atelier Ozenfant, however, one is struck by the importance of the walls. They express protection from the outside environment, although observation from inside is encouraged through the large areas of glass. Le Corbusier's image of a client in these early years is of a contemplative observer somewhat detached from those around him. This image stems both from his actual clientele, who tended toward the intellectual, and his admiration for the monastic life. Wright's clients, on the other hand, were for the most part practical individuals. The distinction, although not great, allows ostensibly poetic differences to be interpreted as prosaic. Consider that although the free-flowing space within both houses is of similar dynamic quality, Le Corbusier tended to mark off special functional areas with screen walls, whereas Wright would have used a subtle modulation of wall or molding. There is in Le Corbusier a distinctly greater orientation to individual activity and privacy. Ideally attuned to dense city life, this quality when transferred to the country as at the Villa Savoie, or even the suburbs as at the Villa Stein, becomes somewhat forced. But even in his city houses, surrounded with their sheltering walls, Le Corbusier encourages outdoor activities on his roof gardens, a sort of controlled dose of nature taken more for reasons of hygiene than for pleasure.

Finally, the related theme of *response to environment* is manifested in the Baker House by Wright's redirection of architectural form toward primitive analogues for shelter, reorganized in the form of structural archetypes for Modern society. The cave, represented by the fireplace, and the tent, represented by the surrounding framework of wood, stucco, and glass, are abstracted and integrated into a contemporary whole that defines man's position in society as tied to a response to nature. The family unit is celebrated, represented by a series of freestanding houses along a common street. The empirical, inclusive twentieth-century mind, evaluating the claims of civilization with objective detachment, therefore settles for a safe, simple, and controlled existence based on its knowledge of and respect for the natural environment.

Far different is the attitude of the Atelier Ozenfant. Instead of protecting itself from the street by a lawn, the house includes a tiny paved courtyard at its front, a microcosmic representation of the traditional French courtyard of the sort of semiprivate space that mediates public and private domains in dense cities. Too small to be satisfactorily occupied by a large family, the house supports the solitary activity of the modern urban individual. The objective rationality expressed in its functional configuration is echoed in its assemblage of standardized building elements as a construction technique. It is poetic in its distance from immediate subjective response and tragic in its success at expressing very personally the impersonality of the modern world.

In considering the position of these two works in history, one is struck by their common attitude toward the past and the future. By denying the architectural systems of the Neoclassicists and revivalists, they break the tradition of justifying the present by pointing to the past. By abstracting and simplifying their formal elements, they bring to architecture the newly developed empiricism that had begun to transform the scholarly, technological, and scientific fields of knowledge. By emphasizing human activity that supports and is supported by the development of the modern world, they assert a new interpretation of the requirements of function. By adopting new attitudes toward construction, they prepare for a future based on mass production and machine fabrication. All these are aspects of what will, in the next chapter, be termed *dynamism,* the acceptance of progress and change.

In addition, both houses favor flexibility of function and construction, and to this extent they are prototypes. They are composites, assemblages of coordinated attitudes held in tension rather than resolved. The twentieth century is welcomed for its wealth of possibilities, for its multifarious energy, and for the thrill of its uncertainty. These are aspects of what will be called *multiplicity,* an acceptance of plurality in modern life.

From a direct, analytic comparison of the works of Frank Lloyd Wright and Le Corbusier, then, a common language can be determined that begins to address the problems and situations and opportunities of the modern world. Although their points of view were different, their vision was shared. The implications of this shared vision will be developed further into a definition of Modernism in architecture, encompassing both Organic and International Style ideas in that it derives from a view of both masters as paragons.

7 Wright and Le Corbusier as Paragons:
Modernism Defined

It should be apparent by now that the change from the eclectic/revivalist architecture of the nineteenth century to what is called Modern in the twentieth represents more than just stylistic development. The nineteenth century for the West was a cultural watershed that may be characterized as a profound change in *scale*. In important cultural and technological realms of thought—science, politics, history—the range of inquiry and the scope of problems perceived became so broad that the hierarchical Classical consensus was stretched beyond endurance. Since the differences between the Organic architecture of Wright and the International Style of Le Corbusier, although themselves describable in terms of style, have been shown to be less significant than the correspondences, then surely a more precise conception of Modernism requires an inclusive vision, a willingness to surrender to the kaleidoscopic fragments of theory and experiment that are the manifestation in substance of the modern world in development. A Modern vision must risk the loss of such Classical holdovers as unity, harmony, and hierarchy so that it may comprehend a different sort of order, derived empirically from an accepting observation of the multifarious phenomena of the modern world.

It has become fashionable to seek the roots of Modernism far back in the past, eighteenth-century France and even sixteenth-century Italy having replaced the late nineteenth century as the happy hunting ground for today's theoreticians. But although surface similarities can certainly be demonstrated, no stylistic change within a culture should be given equal weight to a profound change of cultural values themselves. The transformation of the richly molded surfaces of Hardouin-Mansart into the smooth, abstract envelopes of Boullée has meaning in the context of a major social upheaval, the French Revolution. But it cannot be said to have any connection with the vast demographic, economic, and technological changes of the following century, changes that brought about the modern world. The transition from late baroque to Greek revival occurred at the level of style: Classicism itself was if anything renewed.

Thus, the birth of the modern world must be seen to include the death of the Classical world, for when the Classical consensus finally fell apart, all that was left was a Neoclassical dream. The totality of the conditions that brought all this about is conventionally referred to as the development of an industrialized mass society, which occurred throughout Europe and America in the nineteenth century and which is still occurring in the rest of the world in the twentieth. At the heart of the issue is the general acceptance of an empirical attitude toward knowledge. In the sciences, the expansion of methodology toward observation and the gathering of data that superseded the concentration on speculation and the perfecting of closed logical systems brought about profound changes in attitudes toward reality, truth, and knowledge. It was not long before the new empirically based attitude began to have an affective rather than just speculative involvement with the surrounding world. Mathematics, that most abstract and perfect of intellectual processes, lost its position as the sole basis for scientific reasoning with the birth of a sister science, statistics. Empirical research in medicine brought about the synthesis of biology and chemistry, biochemistry. Archeology and anthropology brought history from the level of myth to the level of science. Metallurgy and applied physics made the technological development of engineering a continuing process. What all this amounted to was a change in the stance of the scientific attitude from a position of speculation about the world to a position of action within the world. For although the immediate position of the empirical observer was one of detachment and disinterest, the net effect of self-consciousness was to engage in a symbiotic and cyclical transformation of the observed environment. This recognition of man's involvement with the environment is a primary condition for Modernism. For, a culture that defines itself by a confident and positive projection of a utopian future, rather than a passive longing for a supposedly ideal past, requires a commitment to action, an acceptance of responsibility for change, and it is precisely this that is the basis for the change from a Classical to a Modern attitude.

The extension of the empirical point of view to the social and political institutions of the eighteenth century eventually brought about the dissolution of hierarchical systems of control and their replacement with coordinated organizations. The very same arrangement of social classes once seen by monarchs of the divine-right ilk as representing a stability defined by God came to be recognized by more detached social observers as the source for enormous strain upon the political institutions of the time, as a force capable of producing chaos unless relieved by some sort of transformation of the governing apparatus. Thus Marx, for one, saw the relationship of social classes not as mutually supportive and interdependent but as a struggle for the possession of the means of production. Flexible systems of government, most notably the English parliamentary system, could adapt themselves enough to avoid total overthrow, although even here the American Revolution cast a premonitory shadow on Enlightenment illusions of eternal empire. Most striking of all, perhaps, is the French replacement of the most absolute of monarchies with a continually changing series of republics, reflecting the shifting balance of power between her newly coordinated social classes. Other governments entered upon long periods of continual change, whether peaceful or violent, which resulted by the beginning of the twentieth century in a number of roughly equivalent political states in Europe, Asia, and the Americas. The old method of extending influence, by direct takeover and control through intimidation and war, was found through the experience of two world wars not to work in the way that it once had. Survival in the twentieth century so far seems to depend upon an uneasy opposition of alliances, changing blocs of power in which supreme control by any one member is impossible.

Along with the transformation of political systems came the growing self-awareness of individual cultures. Empirically minded social critics produced corrected histories, comparative views of other societies, and theories of social reform. Sciences such as economics offered the possibility of recognizing the new technological forces that were reshaping the world. The most obvious symptom of industrialization was the change of scale. Populations exploded, transportation and communication reduced distances, and the leverage of power was vastly increased by accumulations of capital. In Europe, the capital cities were the focus of collision between newly empowered interests. In the United States, industrialization occurred on virgin territory and became absorbed as an integral part of the development of the new nation. By the beginning of the twentieth century, the misalignment between the real world and idealistic interpretations from the Classical point of view had become critical. Only a total and self-conscious break with the past would allow the intellectuals to catch up.

Modernism, then, begins with *a self-conscious break with the past.* Conventionally, *modern* means "of or relating to the present." *Contemporary* is roughly synonymous. But in the early twentieth century, self-consciousness about what was meant by *modern* became so acute that the term applied itself to a specific set of ideas symptomatic of that time. It was the focusing of these ideas that transformed the artistic and intellectual spheres and, finally, the means of communication within society. In light of this, it can be said that Modernism is *a democratic attitude that accepts both change and plurality as determining conditions for phenomena.*

This is to say that Modernism is dependent upon dynamism and multiplicity, which can be shown to underlie the aspects of Modern form discussed in the analysis of the Vitruvian approach in chapter 5. A thoughtful review of the early works of Wright and Le Corbusier will show that these principles actually define the most important similarities between them, as well as distinguish what is different about their work from that which came before. Both principles may be detected separately in past architectures, but it is their mutual interaction that generates Modern architecture.

As perceptively pointed out by Peter Collins,[44] dynamism can be seen as a characteristic of Gothic architecture, which, counter to a Classical expression of harmony and repose, delighted in vertically soaring spaces and forms. It was also an explicit concern of the Futurist architects of the early twentieth century. Dynamism, as far as the present analysis is concerned, means *the expression of growth, change, or movement,* as opposed to the Classical values of harmony, order, and repose. The early work of Wright and Le Corbusier will be considered in light of these three aspects of dynamism.

Patterns of growth appear frequently at the prosaic level in Wright's earliest work. The direct representation of shapes of vegetation occurs in decorative elements such as friezes, windows, and wood carvings. The plant forms are always presented within a strong geometrical framework, however, and it is this increasing abstraction that distinguishes Wright's handling of the theme from the contemporary Art Nouveau movements in Europe, whose own representation of plant forms emphasized particularized free-form growth.

Wright's interest in the geometry underlying patterns of natural growth forged the link between prosaic representation and a much more profound application at the poetic level of the geometric principles that he believed determined the morphology of plant growth. An example of this is the development of fenestration in his Prairie houses. He used stained glass patterns on his windows to allow light to come into the room from outside while maintaining privacy. Typically, the patterned glass was concentrated in the top part of the light, leaving a clear area at the sill for looking out, just at the eye level of a seated person. Thus, the quality of transparency is treated in direct connection with a representational decorative pattern. But at a much deeper level, this method of controlling light was developed by Wright in two distinctive ways. First, at the top edge of his windows, he placed broad outer eaves that penetrate some distance inside the room as well. These served both to cast a deep shadow along the top of the windows from the outside and to reflect a diffused light off the light-painted soffit into the room. Second, he organized his bands of windows into gradually enlarging ranks, low and dark near the central mass of the house, but getting taller and more transparent at the ends of the wings. The stained glass treatment can be seen fully developed in his first Prairie house, the Bradley House of 1900 (fig. 7-1). But the eaves and window bands were experimented with throughout the Prairie period, and by the time the houses reach mature form, around 1908 in the Robie, Roberts, and Baker houses, the stained glass has become almost purely geometric, or even, in the case of the latter two, dispensed with entirely in favor of a simple diagonal lattice pattern. Thus, for Wright the patterns of growth he discerned in nature and celebrated in decoration were later absorbed into his essential vision of the building itself as a living, growing thing. This is the basis for his own concept of the Organic.

Le Corbusier also began with geometrized patterns of vegetation used in a decorative way similar to that of Wright. But he experienced an abrupt change of vision during the lean years of World War I and avoided any gradual assimilation of principles developed through decoration. Rather, he discovered circulation as an independent system, possibly through his design for an abbatoir of about this time. This conception allowed elements of circulation to affect the geometric configuration of the house. It is first apparent in his Atelier Ozenfant of 1922, where the shell-like spiral stair encloses the circulation path at the point of entry. It becomes more developed throughout his houses of the twenties as sections of wall along circulation corridors become more and more responsive to the implied movement, bending back or jutting forth in a particularized Organic compromise in deference to different functions on either side. The culmination of this is the Villa Savoie, where all the building elements join in a symphony of subtle displacements, of shifts and adjustments from a pure Cartesian ideal to something as alive and responsive as the activities within.

In an equally deep and poetic way, Le Corbusier used replication of a single unit to express the possibility of infinite growth, an open-ended system independent of the constraints of proportion. His early buildings are always beginnings, the first fragments of a new vision with the potential for infinite growth through replication.

By *patterns of change* is meant transformations that occur within the experience of the building rather than transformations from the past recorded in the present fabric of the building. With Wright, transformations occur at *every* level of meaning. It is peculiar to his oeuvre that so many symmetrical plans are entered or approached off the axis of symmetry. Typical of such masterworks as the Darwin Martin House, the Coonley House, the Larkin Building, and Unity Temple, circulation paths off the main axes result in an impression of dynamic stretching and pulling of architectural elements as one approaches and enters; this impression suddenly snaps into resolution as one senses the symmetrical organization. One activity is in this way given primary importance, occupying the central space in a symmetrical *parti* (the church at Unity Temple, the workroom at Larkin, the living rooms of the houses). Throughout the process of approach, entry, and activity, of course, many other transformations are taking place: light to dark to light, openness to pressure to expansion, exposure to protection.

In a Le Corbusier house, the abrupt penetration of the facade is just the first step in a series of spatial transformations that gradually lead upward to the protected roof garden and the sky. Darkness gradually gives way to lightness, compression to expansion as the upward path is traversed. The clearest example of this progress and its culmination is, of course, the Villa Savoie with its ramp to the sky. This is reminiscent of Wright's own sky-caves, although he generally used the type for public buildings rather than for private houses.

Most characteristic of the expression of dynamism are patterns of movement. Indeed, implied motion is at the core of many concepts that have been traditionally represented as characteristic of Modern architecture, such as *open planning, charged space,* and *art of the machine.* At the prosaic level, both Wright and Le Corbusier emphasized line over surface or mass, line being the geometric element most basic to an expression of movement. Beaux-Arts buildings are characterized by richly rendered surfaces and complex, broken outlines that offer a static expression of weight and mass, often quite different from the cleaner, lighter treatment of line in the Classic originals. The soaring vertical emphasis of Gothic was derived from a continuity of vertical lines

7-1. Wright: Bradley House, Kankakee, Illinois, 1900.

against broken horizontals. As has been mentioned previously, the simplicity of form said to be characteristic of Modern architecture is actually a result of maintaining the integrity of lines and edges.

But at the deeper level, both Wright and Le Corbusier expressed movement by emphasizing circulation. One of the first examples of this was Wright's Darwin Martin House in its original state. As one turned to enter the front door, a continuous vista was presented through the main living areas and beyond, outside again along a covered walk to the conservatory at the end of the garden. This celebration of path was picked up by Le Corbusier in the Villa Savoie, although there it is folded back upon itself as a ramp rising through the two levels of the house. As has been discussed previously, this theme remained basic to their work, culminating in Wright's Guggenheim Museum, which is almost all path, and Le Corbusier's High Courts building at Chandigarh, where the Savoie ramp is expanded.

It should be clear from this brief exposition that dynamism is of primary importance in the early careers of both architects. Their rejection of the static, balanced esthetic of Neoclassicism was complete and conscious. They recognized the modern world to be one of change and motion and, confronting the dread with which many faced the unpredictability of a society in flux, proposed in its stead a celebration of the excitement and energy they foresaw for the future.

The term *multiplicity* is used here to denote a very particular characteristic of twentieth-century art. It has to do with intersection and collision, with things that occupy the same place at the same time, with the interaction of equivalent, independent systems. It might be said to be the space element that corresponds to the time element of dynamism. Something like multiplicity can be found in the interpenetrating spaces of baroque architecture, manifested in a sort of overlay of different geometric shapes, each still recognizable. But here there is always some all-encompassing ordering principle or hierarchy of spaces, perhaps a regular grid or clear subordination of complex shapes to simpler ones. Multiplicity in a more Modern sense can be found in the Picturesque style popular among nineteenth-century architects. The composite effect of an agglomeration of unrelated parts over time, seen, for example, in such archetypal buildings as the medieval monastery of Mont-Saint-Michel, was widely admired and copied in the last century. But again, the added-on parts, whether they were designed together or not, reflected some hierarchy of value applied to the functions they housed. A *focal point* of the composition would be created: a stair tower or great hall, for instance.

The attitude of Wright and Le Corbusier as they began the important periods of their early careers was quite different from this. Wright's Prairie buildings always express the intersection of several building systems, designed with such coherence of detail that each has a strong aura of independence. The basic Wrightian systems—masonry, window, and roof— have already been examined for their symbolic representation of basic natural elements: respectively, the earth, forest, and sky. In fact the examination of a plan of one of Wright's Prairie houses (see fig. 6-2a) reveals the three systems distinguished graphically: the solid blacks of masonry masses against the light double lines of the window and framing, with the dashed outlines of the roofs above. Although all three enclose the same space, they never quite coincide. This sense of disjuncture is experienced within the building. On entering, one usually first passes under the roof edge, then slips past a masonry parapet, and finally through a door or French window. All detailing and planning of the house supports the distinction that is kept between these systems, from moldings that often do not follow edges (and even leave the plane of the wall surface) to reveals that express actual breaks within a system as it responds to another. For the systems are made to interrelate: to interrupt, overcome, and impose upon each other in ways that express Wright's vision of organic growth in the natural world. This has been discussed already with respect to the Johnson Wax Headquarters.

Le Corbusier also recognized and expressed equivalent independent systems. In his plans one can read three of the basic four: the grid of columns, the screen walls, and the service core, none of which are exactly the same in configuration and all of which interrelate in the same fragmented, unpredictable way that Wright's do. The other system, the ribbon windows, works similarly in elevation. For Le Corbusier, modern life was a composite of different related but independent activities, each of which made claims upon the building designed to house it. It is in the careful recognition of the independence of these activities that Le Corbusier's architecture achieves profound meaning for the modern world. He wanted to express the great social forces endemic to mass civilization, particularly the blindness of standardized production to decorative refinement and elaborate detailing.

Thus, multiplicity is the simultaneous occupation of space by a number of different systems, each having some independent meaning outside the context of the building itself. It is the expression of this independent meaning that acknowledges the standardization of function and construction that is characteristic of the modern world and so manifests itself in form and iconography. Such phenomena as *charged space* and *transparency* are aspects of mul-

tiplicity expressed through systems of building elements. Like dynamism, it absolutely opposes the Classical values of harmony, repose, and hierarchical order with dissonance, movement, and coordinated superimposition.

In conclusion, then, Modernism in architecture can be characterized by two attitudes: dynamism and multiplicity, which together presuppose a rejection of the past as a justification for the hierarchical interpretation of culture. It has been demonstrated that the architectures of Wright and Le Corbusier have this much in common, at least in their early careers. In order to develop the idea of Modernism for twentieth-century architecture, a definition of Modern architecture might be suggested thus: *Architecture is the process by which places occupied by the mind are made into spaces habitable by the body.*

In accepting architecture as a *process,* one acknowledges the dynamic conception of the world as a place of movement, growth, and change. The openness of such a definition to possibility and variation is in accord with the principle of multiplicity. It allows for the social process of architecture as well as for the personal process of the architect. In fact, the interaction of the architect with the systems of technological, social, and economic possibilities in his culture is an analogue to the more general issue of the relation of modern man to his culture.

By this definition, too, the work of architecture becomes a *social product,* a result of the process, a visible and tangible record of the forces involved in its creation. Evaluation of a work of architecture, then, is based upon how well it reflects that which determines its existence. The architect's responsibility is limited to the extent of his control: The possibilities for architecture in any context are constrained by the intentions of the sources of power controlling its production.

Recognition of the work of architecture as a social product allows for the identification of a range of Modernist possibilities. The great sources of power, the corporations, institutions, and governmental bodies, produce conservative works of architecture, works that partake more than others of the past. The Classical values of harmony, repose, order, and stability, remaining in Modern thought at the level of wish or dream, are most important to them. Small independent businesses, institutions, and individuals tend to be more experimental and are often willing to take chances, albeit of moderate dimensions. The important built works of Modern architecture seem to fall mostly within this category. The most radical work, usually existing only on paper, is generated by architects and critics and—most significantly—is always characterized by a visionary or forward-looking quality. Many scholars have recognized this utopian element in Modern architecture, and it is of course connected with the rejection of the past, in distinct contrast to Classical architecture.

According to the definition above, an important distinction has been made between *image,* i.e., the places inhabited by the mind, and the *execution* that leads to the spaces habitable by the body. In this way, the imagination of the architect is recognized for its role in the architectural process. The modern world, with its high level of technological sophistication and complicated building programs, demands particular flexibility in the architect's imagination if a project is to be built as architecture. How the architect responds to programmatic, economic, technical, and political influences during the development of the project will determine the architectural quality of the final work. The image itself can be given up if these influences are seen as unbreakable constraints. The result of this is indifferent, meaningless buildings, however correctly they represent the social influences on them. If the architect is very determined, the image can be maintained at the cost of repressing the manifestations of social influences. Neither of these approaches can bring fine results, since the balance between image and execution is lost. A third approach is to see external influences as opportunities for enriching the image, perhaps even changing it substantially. This is the point of view from which Wright and Le Corbusier saw the esthetic and iconographic possibilities in standardization.

The significance of the architectural product will be determined by the imaginative range of the architect. Both Wright and Le Corbusier derived images from what they saw as proto- or archetypal building forms: the shelter and cloister, the cave and tent. They also used natural forms: Wright's plant shapes and Le Corbusier's anthropomorphic masses. They continually enriched their imagery by returning to these basic sources as they developed their styles. It is a gauge of greatness that they looked outside architecture itself for images, unlike many architects whose main inspiration seems to come from the buildings of others. Architecture turned in upon itself becomes hermetic, unreal, not related to the outside world. The empty quality that is so strikingly common to much eclectic and International Style architecture, different as these are, is a result of such introversion. It is testimony to the statures of Wright and Le Corbusier, therefore, that they did not seek direct influence from each other's work but followed their own paths into the same territory at different points in their careers. Their work would not be so comprehensive if this were not true.

What architects can claim to have in common with other artists, then, is the relevance of the sources of their imagery, the strength of their connection with the processes of the modern world, and their willingness to accept legitimate influence from the larger culture in developing their imagery. The image determines the content of all artistic expression: It is the connection between the architect and observer. If architects are to share their vision with others, they must speak an understandable language, one that offers a discovered simplicity rather than befuddling complexity.

For if the image is complicated to begin with, what will happen as the modifications, deletions, and additions endemic to the construction process have their effect? The inherent multiplicity of the architectural product stems from these forces and it is in recognition of this that the finest architects of Modernism have invariably relied upon simple images. Wright used multiples of basic geometric figures—squares, circles, triangles, and hexagons—for the clearest representation of his caves, tents, cloisters, and shelters. Le Corbusier began initially with archetypal structural forms—the box, the column, the roof slab—and assembled them into composites similar, as has been shown, to Wright's.

Changes occur at each of the Vitruvian levels during the design development and construction of a work of architecture. Functional changes come about with program additions and modifications; cost estimates begin to affect the design as alternatives are explored. Technological changes result from the selection of structural and mechanical systems whose most favorable application requires modification of the scheme. Formal changes improve the clarity of the expression as the work is considered from various points of view.

If the image is kept clearly in view and a dialogue that elaborates upon the initial meaning is developed, the result is an enrichment of content in the finished work. Each of Wright's Prairie houses is the product of a simple, hipped-roof pavilion with a central fireplace that is exploded, molded, and shaped according to the social and environmental exigencies of its site and program. In the pages of the first volume (1910–29) of Le Corbusier's *Oeuvre Complète,* one can trace the development of the Dom-Ino house system through increasingly sophisticated variations to the ultimate Villa Savoie. It is in this sense that architecture becomes a truly dynamic process. The building as organism responds to the forces of its creation just as the natural object carries the marks of the universal forces of nature. This can be confirmed by a comparison of the late work of Wright and Le Corbusier, where it will be seen that in architecture, if not after all in biology, ontogeny recapitulates phylogeny.

8 Wright and Le Corbusier as Confederates:
Late Work in Comparison

With dynamism and multiplicity seen to be the determinants of Modernism in twentieth-century architecture, the later careers of Wright and Le Corbusier can be examined from a common point of view, showing that each continued his development of a comprehensive Modernism by exploring, at least in part, what had previously been the theoretical domain of the other. It has already been shown in chapter 1 that Wright adopted many of the stylistic themes of the International Style in the late 1930s. In his careful selection of these themes, he made them his own and, considering how much the International Style derived from Wright's early work, the result was not at all a divergence from his former path but rather a leap forward to a control that very few architects have ever achieved over their designs. Once the initial tidal wave of new work had crested, by 1940, Wright in his seventies condensed and enriched the iconographic content of his work. The many houses he designed and built in the last twenty years of his life are sketches, gestures tossed off his drawing board, that exhibit precision of scale and clarity of systems rather than voluptuous detail. The brilliance and subtlety of the result can be seen in Wingspread, the house built for Herbert Johnson between 1938 and 1940 near Racine, Wisconsin. The largest house that Wright ever built, Wingspread is an example of his insistence on intimacy of scale and integrity of materials. Quiet reference is made to the elegance of the red-painted concrete floors by the entry foyer, which has a marble floor of the same shade of red. The only ornament in the house is a tiny thread of repeated squares in wood, which appears here and there, sometimes defining a joint between materials and other times simply drawn across a surface (fig. 8-1). This simple line, related to but independent of the other elements of the house, is the culmination of the elaborate wood strips that outline the spaces of the early Prairie houses.

Wright's public buildings have this same easy clarity. Even the question of ornament itself is raised in his last masterpiece, the Marin County Civic Center (see fig. 8-10a). The arches of the entrances at grade are gradually reduced in size up the side of the building until, at the eaves of the roof, they become decorative cuts holding small gold-colored spheres at the scale of the human hand. These

8-1. Wright: Wingspread, Wind Point, Wisconsin, 1937.

appear to weigh down the greatest arc of all, the swelling curve of the thin roof membrane. The question raised is which of these arcs are ornamental and which architectural?

For Le Corbusier, the change came after the fallow years of World War II, during which very little of anything was built. Many of his famous houses of the 1920s had deteriorated, partly due to neglect, as at Poissy, but mostly because they were poorly detailed for weathering. Another contributing factor to his stylistic change was his extensive concern with town planning during the 1930s. As he confronted a series of real planning projects for cities in France and South America, he gradually moved away from the formalism of La Ville Contemporaine and toward a recognition of the patterns of natural growth.

His final move from the abstract Cartesian geometry of the 1920s was his development of the Modulor in the 1940s. This was a system of measurement and proportion based ostensibly on the Golden Mean, but it also derives from what is known in mathematics as the Fibonacci series, a progression of numbers that has been discovered to be a major determinant of growth in nature. At the same time as the development of the Modulor came a new interest in the patterns of materials, mostly the imprint of wooden form boards in concrete but also the grain and finish of wood itself. Both these concerns were eschewed by the International Style and celebrated by Wright in his early career.

Another development in Le Corbusier's late career was the adoption of shapes characteristic of other arts. His sculptures in wood appear to have influenced such buildings as the chapel at Ronchamp. Many of the free-form curves so characteristic of his later plans—difficult to describe precisely for construction— have the gestural quality of shapes from his paintings. And his window walls were often detailed with a mullion spacing derived from the intervals of the musical scale, in which he was said to be assisted by a professor of music from the Sorbonne.

In spite of individual differences between him and Wright, an overall mutual correspondence can be sensed, never material but somehow in the air in the 1940s and 1950s. Although there is no documentary evidence that they took much notice of each other, it would be naive to deny that they were in some way aware of each other's work. At any rate, it has been shown that Wright intensified his interest in abstract surfaces and masses, in machine construction and in planning grids—triangles and circles as well as squares and rectangles. Le Corbusier, for his part, became interested in the patterns of organic growth and in the tactile and decorative qualities of natural materials. More important, at last, than evidence of direct mutual correspondence is the recognition that they were on the same track, that what they expressed as the determining aspects of the modern world were essentially the same. These, of course, have been identified here as dynamism and multiplicity, and these aspects can be discovered in their later work through the four-part Vitruvian approach developed in chapter 5.

Fortunately for this analysis, the case can be made that both Wright and Le Corbusier each managed to get constructed a single culminating masterpiece toward the end of their careers, a building that sums up much of what they were trying to say throughout their lives. Wright's masterpiece is the Guggenheim Museum, designed between 1943 and 1956 and completed just after his death in 1959. Le Corbusier's is the monastery of La Tourette, designed between 1950 and 1955 and completed in 1959 within months of the Guggenheim. In the following analysis, these two buildings will be continually referred to, along with other examples that reflect particular aspects of their late styles.

The Guggenheim Museum in New York represents Wright at his most controlled (fig. 8-2a). It has a quality of concentration in its reprisal of virtually all the major themes of his career. The first characteristic of Modern form—*integrity of surfaces and edges*—is exemplified at the Guggenheim with a precision that is the culmination of seventy years of architectural practice. All surfaces are rendered smooth and off-white with the exception of the fascia of the roof monitor of the cylindrical office wing to the north and the screen at the east of this, a remnant of a proposed office block that was never built. As a result, the composition of masses whose intersection is the museum itself is entirely clear and readable from three sides and—important in a high-rise city—from the top. Treatment of the edges is particularly careful. The clean, sharp arrises of the spiral ramp show it to be, both inside and out, a curving tray that fills the space formed by the intersection of two coaxial cones, one increasing upward and the other increasing downward. Clear representation of the different floors of the minor office wing is given through the use of different geometric figures in plan: a cylinder, a truncated pyramid, and a regular polygonal prism. The suppressed edges of the curved corners of the Grand Gallery wing on the south subordinate this mass to the spiral cone rising above it. Finally, there is the precise expression of structural webs, service shaft tubes, and circulation parapets that compose the interior.

At La Tourette, there is the same concern for sharp and clear definition of building masses that seem to fill geometric solids in space (fig. 8-2b). Even the balconies attached to the dormitory wings can be read as a solid lamination applied to the main block. Smaller geometric solids—the pyramid over the minor chapel, the hexagonal prisms over the sacristy, the truncated cones over the grotto—are applied to reinforce the reading of a composition of precisely defined masses, intersecting to produce the monastery. Structural webs and service shaft tubes are represented in a manner quite similar to that of the Guggenheim. Thus the overall reading—a rectangular mass almost, but not quite, closing a U of three similar masses—is unequivocally stated. The homogeneity of the surface rendering, as at the Guggenheim, allows for a controlled definition of minor incidents in the masses, such as the distinction between the three systems of fenestration—the balconies, the harmonically distributed slots of glass, and the ribbon windows of the interior—used to represent functional distinctions, as it is at the Guggenheim.

The second characteristic of Modern form—*generation of a system of spatial cells formed by perpendicular transparent planes*—is handled at the Guggenheim with a transcendence that gives the museum claim to being the penultimate Modern space. In plan, the museum begins with simple distribution of spaces on a square grid that respects the alignment of Manhattan streets (fig. 8-3a). It is upon the careful destruction of this grid that Wright's whole effort depends. The Guggenheim was originally planned to display the largest collection of Kandinsky paintings in the world. Kandinsky was one of the first Non-Objective painters and his works tend to be spatial, evoking a sort of architecture from abstract figures and brush strokes. Recognizing this, it can be assumed that Wright's intent was to "erase" the architecture of the building itself in order to allow for the greatest possible involvement in the paintings. The perception of space—as has been proposed as a result of experimentation—is based on a sort of mapping apparatus in the brain that records incre-

8-2a. Wright: Solomon Guggenheim Museum, New York, 1943–56.

8-2b. Le Corbusier: Couvent de la Tourette, Arbresle, 1950–55.

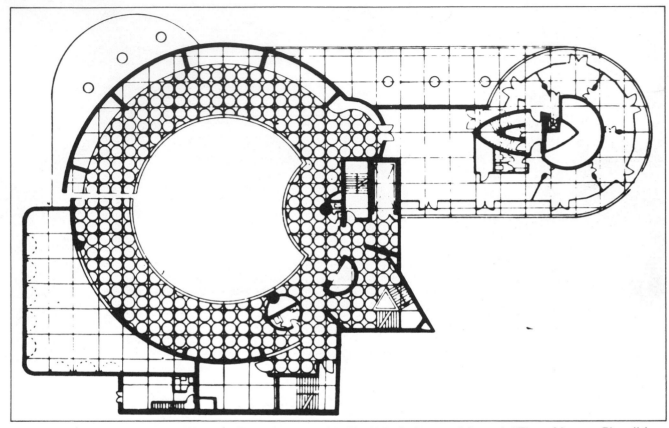

8-3a. Wright: plan, Guggenheim Museum. (From *Perspecta 16: The Yale Architectural Journal,* "Thirty Museum Plans," by Kirk Train, p. 157. MIT Press, 1980.)

ments of space according to the three cardinal axes of Cartesian space, two horizontal and one vertical. The generation of space in the Guggenheim Museum is an intentional removal of all references to the determining Cartesian grid, resulting in the notorious vertigo experienced along its ramp. There is a contrast between the image of an endless curving path in space and the punctuation of circulation elements that signal repeated circular motion. Added to this is the kinesthetically experienced pull of gravity that reinforces the drive down the slope of the ramp. Along with the curved and slanting walls, the diminishing width of the ramp is finally countered with a single Cartesian reference—the flat main floor and vertical axis of the spiral—that restores perceptual cues to the mind. Thus, a walk down the Guggenheim ramp is a journey into a surreal dynamic of tangible space in which the human mind is helpless and

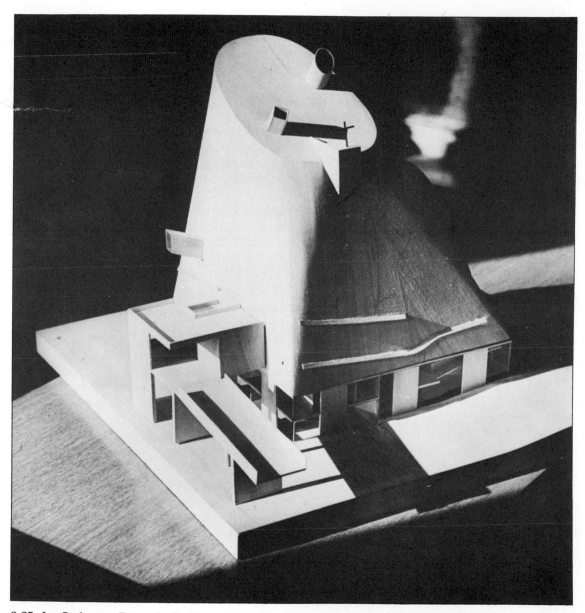

8-25. Le Corbusier: Eglise de St. Pierre de Firminy-Vert, 1960, project. (Courtesy of Fondation Le Corbusier.)

speaker and on the natural landscape beyond. The duality of man and nature is again explicit.

In the Beth Sholom Synagogue, many images are evoked: the Ark of the Covenant, a mountain, a primitive temple. But one must be sure to recognize Wright's interest in the wigwam shape representing the archetypal tent. The sense of climbing a mountain to a kind of valley in the clouds is particularly pronounced. Pure light, filtered through the translucent roof panels, falls upon the congregation and the effect is quieter than at the other churches, solemn without being somber and more focused upon the ritual.

At the Greek Orthodox church, reference is made to Byzantine architecture in the cruciform plan and the blue spherical saucer dome. The church is dark, lit through a clerestory low at the edges of the roof saucer, and the congregation, because of its seating configuration, is probably more aware of itself than at the other three churches. The result is introspective in a communal way, assisting the individual in becoming aware of membership in a religious community.

Le Corbusier's chapel at Ronchamp, designed for pilgrims, calls attention to itself with an isolation and plasticity reminiscent of the Annie Pfeiffer Chapel. Although the interior is a surprise not anticipated by the approach outside, it is dark and introspective. The church is designed for the private contemplation of the individual pilgrim and not for congregational services, which may be held outside on the grass facing the exterior altar provided for this.

The church at La Tourette is similarly introspective, designed for the singing of masses by priests rather than for a lay congregation. The windowless interior almost shuts out the day, and it is the sculptural emphasis on the symbolic parts of the church—the sacristy, chapels, altar, nave, and choir—that is used to evoke spiritual concentration.

Le Corbusier's church at Firminy-Vert, designed for a parish, will have much of the external presence of the Beth Sholom Synagogue: a tent over a cave. The lighting will focus dramatically on the altar, emphasizing the performance of the mass, and the congregation will not have much of a sense of itself because of the steeply tiered seating. It will be a theater for the acting out of the religious service, a much less contemplative space than his other two churches.

Dynamism and multiplicity are apparent in these seven churches. Wright sets up conflicting centers and axes, carefully balancing them so that no single hierarchy is established. At the Annie Pfeiffer Chapel and the First Unitarian Church, this supports contemplation of the dualism of man and nature. At the Beth Sholom Synagogue, it creates a symbolic journey by which a place of pure spiritual light can be reached. At the Greek Orthodox church, the forces are greatly diminished and the experience is quieter and more traditional. Le Corbusier achieves dynamic opposition of functional and environmental systems by delineating conflicting axes. At Ronchamp the deeply contemplative focus on the crucifix is contradicted by the brilliant shaft of natural light at the corner. At La Tourette the opposition of the monastic choir in the nave and the chapels of the sanctuary beyond the altar evokes consideration of the individual and communal aspects of religious brotherhood. At Firminy-Vert the vertical axis of the tall enclosing walls is contradicted by the angled shaft of sunlight streaming in from above.

At the prosaic level of iconographic content, then, the seven late churches of Wright and Le Corbusier exhibit similar concerns for an expressive symbology appropriate to the particular religious character of each one. From both the functional and the purposive standpoints, these buildings demonstrate profound similarities between the images selected by the two architects as well as between their methods of execution. It is in the places inhabited by the mind, however, even more than the spaces inhabited by the body, that one finds the essence of their common vision. Caves and tents, cloisters and shelters can be recognized from the foregoing analysis as the determining images for these churches, but further exploration into the *poetic* level of iconographic content will best be served by a look at the most important building type for both men: the dwelling.

The many houses designed by Frank Lloyd Wright can be organized, for the most part, into four iconographic types, each representing a particular combination of cloister and shelter, the two functional prototypes found in his work. The later Prairie house represents, of course, shelter in the form of an open pavilion protected above from rain and the scorching sun. But it also represents an inverted cloister, a framework for basic human activity that is open on at least two sides to society at large and that therefore implies a generic connection between family activity and social interaction. This was identified and examined earlier in the analysis of the Baker House of 1909, but it is iconographically much clearer in the later Prairie-type houses. The most explicit statement of the inverted cloister is in the great house for Herbert Johnson, Wingspread, one of the key works of the mid-1930s that established the parameters of Wright's late career. The radiating arms of Wingspread form four half-courts, open to the landscape on two sides and bounded by functional areas on the other two (fig. 8-26). Each half-court has a generic function: arrival, departure, and greeting;

8-26. Wright: Johnson House (Wingspread).

recreation; cultivation of the land; and family interaction. This organization is repeated in the central hall where corresponding functions are provided with adjoining spaces around the massive multiple fireplace.

A very similar organization is apparent in the Reisley House of 1951, a typical late Prairie house. Here, two of Wingspread's four cloister wings, the master bedroom wing and the children's bedroom wing, are laid out at a sixty-degree angle to each other. Between the two are a hexagonal living room, defined with a sheltering pyramidal roof, and family dining/kitchen area. Both wings connect directly with exterior

8-27. Wright: Reisley House, Pleasantville, New York, 1951.

spaces carefully located and arranged to correspond with the activity inside: the greeting and arrival porte cochere; the dining terrace tucked immediately behind this; the private garden up a flight of steps from the dining terrace, which then gives access to a roof deck; the living room terrace on the other side of the house; the lawn adjacent to this terrace along the children's bedrooms; and the private balcony off the master bedroom suite, looking out at the rest of the neighborhood and arrival road, but secluded from the other outdoor spaces (fig. 8-27).

A somewhat different attitude is characteristic of the second type, the Usonian house. Here, a sheltering wall is used to distinguish strictly private areas from the public approach. Family activity is treated as something separate from the life of the greater surrounding society. At the same time, protection

from nature is implied in the simple sheltering roof slab and the expansive glass walls that open to the inner court. This makes it a fragmented rather than an inverted cloister, since the protection from the outside world is retained. The Lloyd Lewis House is an example of this configuration, as is the later Glore House near Chicago (fig. 8-28).

A third iconographic type is defined by the block type houses, first developed in the 1920s but continued in various forms throughout Wright's career, culminating in the build-it-yourself Usonian Automatic of the 1950s. The protective nature of the thick, enclosing walls is emphasized, resulting in an introverted, self-absorbed environment suited to an individual living alone, Aline Barnsdall or Mrs. Millard, for example. This attitude is also used in environments that are dramatic but hostile, such as the ramped David Wright House or the Harold Price House in Arizona. These houses often show the intensely cloistered interiors of Wright's sky-cave public buildings, as can be seen at the Friedman House in Pleasantville, New York.

A fourth type is represented by the solar hemicycle. Here, family interaction in nature is the whole focus of the house, buried as it is against the wind and the surrounding environment. In a sense, this house *is* a cloister, the opposite of the Prairie house in its expression of protection from the side along with openness to the sunlight above. The sheltering function is achieved here almost entirely through the use of the cloister form, which itself was developed originally for work places, not houses. The solar hemicycle type, therefore, represents a sort of culmination in Wright's production of houses. All four house types were built through the 1950s and demonstrate the range of Wright's thinking and the precision with which he was able to convey meaning through architecture.

160 Wright and Le Corbusier as Confederates

8-28. Wright: Glore House, Lake Forest, Illinois, 1951.

Each of the house types came about from Wright's interpretation of the interaction of the three realms of the individual, the family, and the society. The dynamism of change is embodied in the transitions that occur perceptually as one walks through the spaces of the house, transitions that perhaps reflect different attitudes toward the three realms mentioned above, or that symbolize the changes likely to occur within them over time as family members come and go. Certainly, the incorporation of typical house patterns into his other buildings indicates the comprehensiveness of Wright's attitudes toward human function. The inverted cloister form of Wingspread can be found in most of his mass housing projects, from the small Suntop Terrace of 1938 near Philadelphia to the Price Tower and Crystal Heights project. But beyond this, Wright's meaning stems from the interaction between the three realms, never totally resolved but always held in tension. This, of course, is a manifestation of multiplicity.

Le Corbusier built far fewer houses than Wright did. His two types, the Catalan vault house and the studio-house, are based on shelter and cloister images, respectively. Similar in many ways to Wright's Prairie house, the Catalan vault shelter type continued to be built throughout Le Corbusier's career, as the Maisons Jaoul and Villa Sarabhai of the 1950s attest. The type has a horizontally oriented connection with the outside, which, as with Wright's houses, encourages interaction with others rather than introspection. This is possibly the explanation for Le Corbusier's choice of the type for the Maisons Jaoul. The site is cramped and urban, particularly suited for his other type, the vertical studio-house. But the fact that two houses were called for—different branches of the same family were to be separately accommodated—implies a ground-floor relationship, a sort of semiprivate zone between the houses that would not be accomplished with the strictly private studio-house type. So the Catalan vaults were stacked, somewhat awkwardly, in an experiment of interaction between the two houses. One thinks of Wright's Martin/Barton houses in Buffalo, New York.

If the vaults are aligned more than two deep, very private introspective spaces are formed in the central area, creating a virtual cloister similar to Wright's block-type house. This can be seen at the Villa Sarabhai. Other similarities can be found in the villa's thick, masonry walls and roof and in its darkness. When the roofs are planted, as at the Sarabhai House, it begins to recall Wright's solar hemicycle type, also laid out with particular respect for the natural environment.

The raised-cloister type of house began as a studio-house in the 1920s. It became generalized in response to Le Corbusier's insistence on the importance of contemplation and solitude for the individual in the modern world. The closed service spaces of the ground floor are protected from the surrounding neighborhood. These houses always incorporate a ramp that induces a sense of blossoming upward of space. The higher up one climbs, the more open the house becomes, until, at the roof level, sometimes screened with freestanding walls and sometimes sheltered with a light parasol roof, there are open terraces—here called raised cloisters. The type was originally designed for the dense building sites of the city, and the one for Dr. Currutchet at La Plata, Argentina, is a late example of this. But it was used in the country as well, for example in the Villa Savoie at Poissy and in the Villa Shodan in India. The variation in sheltering screens or roofs at the terraces allowed for different degrees of connection with the environment and with nature. An interesting comparison could be made with Wright's spiral block-type house for David Wright in Arizona.

Le Corbusier extended both house types to mass housing. The famous Unité d'Habitation built at Marseilles and elsewhere has the ground-level protection and roof top openness of the raised-cloister type. A scheme for the extension of the Catalan vault type was the Roq et Rob project of 1949 for Cap Martin on the French Riviera. Maximum privacy and introspection were achieved with the tight packing of the longitudinal blocks, appropriate for affluent weekenders who probably would have little desire to form a neighborhood among themselves, a transformation from shelter into cloister reminiscent of Wright's solar hemicycle scheme.

The work of Le Corbusier, finally, exhibits a recognition of cloister and shelter and creates precise and subtle shades of meaning through combinations of these two archetypes. All of this, of course, is quite close to what Wright was doing in his own houses. The most significant difference lies in the social levels upon which each focuses: Le Corbusier upon the individual and his interaction with a larger society; Wright on the family.

And yet, how much of a difference does this finally make? At the deepest, most poetic level of iconography, Wright and Le Corbusier were dealing with the same tensions, conflicts, and discordances. They proposed an architecture for the modern world based upon the collision of possibilities—as represented by interacting structural archetypes and functional prototypes—rather than any single, perfected building type. They foresaw a world of contingency, of risk, of change; a world that could best be experienced through a feat of surrender. The sense of tragedy that haunts much of Le Corbusier's late work is related to a mourning of the loss of a Classically ordered past, whereas the sunny optimism of Wright's work confirms a recognition of dynamism and multiplicity as older even than civilization itself, thus enabling the modern individual to experience at a deeper level than ever before the generating energy of nature. It is fitting at this point, therefore, to examine the implications of the elements common to both masters for a Modern conception of style, acknowledging them in these terms as counterparts.

9 Wright and Le Corbusier as Counterparts:
Style from the Inclusive Point of View

The similarity of so many esthetic themes in the work of Frank Lloyd Wright and Le Corbusier, the near identity of so many of their concerns, the inability of critics to define pertinent stylistic differences between them—all this indicates that theoretical approaches originally developed to explain the architecture of the past fall short in dealing with Modern architecture. It might be reasonably claimed that Modern architecture is still too current for the detached consideration demanded by traditional scholarship. But one suspects that enough time has passed by now, in the late twentieth century, to allow a view more judicious than has been developed so far.

One might further suspect that the continuing problem of Modern style for critics is rooted in the very nature of Modernism itself. It has been shown that an understanding of Modernism requires giving up hierarchical frameworks of thought and adopting in their place an empirical and inclusive point of view. What this implies in the realm of scholarship traditionally pursued is far from clear and merits extended consideration. It is a problem familiar to the leading art scholars of the twentieth century. Meyer Schapiro, in his seminal article on style, writes:

The modern experience of stylistic variability and of the unhomogeneous within an art style will perhaps lead to a more refined conception of style. It is evident, at any rate, that the conception of style as a visibly unified constant rests upon a particular norm of stability of style and shifts from the large to the small forms, as the whole becomes more complex.[45]

There is a case, then, for the view that the concept of style itself, along with the arts and the intellectual stance of criticism, has changed in the modern world.

For style as "a visibly unified constant" demands a single coherent system of values. That which a culture values most, defines itself by, or sees as universal is embodied in the style of its art. This is the basis on which styles of the past have been defined, both by the historians of the nineteenth and twentieth centuries and by writers and thinkers contemporary with the styles themselves. The key to this idea resides in the term *unified*. Unity implies correspondence between different aspects of a culture, a focus of concern in its art that can be seen as generally congruent with the politics, religion, and general philosophical beliefs held by cultural leaders. But it also implies exclusion of ideological strains that cannot be made to fit. As long as one set of values can be made dominant, and apparent to those who care about it, the framework will hold.

Certain characteristics of such a conception of style can be discerned in the cultures of the past. It has been frequently pointed out by scholars that styles often have distinct early, middle, and late stages. The early stage of a style can be termed *developmental,* since it is then that opposing possibilities for ideology sort themselves out. The art of such a period tends to be experimental, rough, and open. A culture at this phase is consciously seeking new universals and, consequently, there is a great deal of freedom for artists to experiment with different ideas. Yet there is no single foundation for artistic thought. Historical periods of this type could be exemplified by twelfth-century France, fourteenth-century Florence, and sixteenth-century England.

The middle phase of stylistic progress can be termed *operative.* Art of this type tends to be refined, simple, and purist. It reflects a culture that is confident of its values and that offers clear guidelines for art. Artists make cogent and lucid explorations of commonly held principles and produce an art that is easily understood by their own culture and most apparent to later historians. The early-thirteenth-century cathedrals of northern France, the architecture of Bramante, and the Jacobean country houses of Restoration England can be cited as examples of the operative phases of their styles.

The late phase of a style might be called *restrictive.* Such art is sophisticated, troubled, and rich in dis-cursive detail. The framework that supported the operative phase becomes a cage against which artists must struggle to express their ideas. It is a time when a culture has doubt about its existing values. These values are antagonistic to artists, who compete with each other in ideological ferment. One can detect such circumstances in the Flamboyant art of fourteenth-century France, in the architecture of Michelangelo, and in the late baroque architecture of England.

Such a formulation is of course simplistic. But this comes at least in part with the tendency toward exclusiveness in defining traditionally unified styles. The complex, critical, and sophisticated theories of the twentieth century are a far cry indeed from the simpler explanations of earlier thinkers, not because the scholars of the twentieth century are so much smarter but because the art audience itself is so much more intellectual in its response to contemporary culture. A truly unified style, as so many were in the past, does not call for an elaborate theoretical superstructure. It does not need to be explained to its audience. If a culture is seeking unified, unchanging values, the three-part stylistic pattern described above will naturally develop in its art. Schapiro writes:

Such styles are the most fascinating to historians and philosophers, who admire in this great spectacle of unity the power of a guiding idea or attitude to impose a common form upon the most varied contexts. The dominant style-giving force is identified by some historians with a world outlook common to the whole society; by others with a particular institution, like the church or the absolute monarchy, which under certain conditions becomes the source of a universal viewpoint and the organizer of all cultural life. This unity is not necessarily organic; it may be likened also, perhaps, to that of a machine with limited freedom of motion; in a complex organism the parts are unlike and the integration is more a matter of functional interdependence than of the repetition of the same pattern in all the organs.[46]

Here is identified a deep cultural yearning for hierarchy, a compulsion toward unity. Scholarship itself, stemming from the medieval urge to explain every phenomenon with a single overriding idea, partakes of this attitude.

It is no wonder, then, that a higher value is usually placed by scholars on art of the operative phase of a style. This is correctly interpreted as a time of relative harmony within a culture, whether it is symptomatic of general contentment of the citizens or of ultimate totalitarian control. Since such art is clear and easy to understand, it lends itself to discourse. Also, it must be kept in mind that this sort of art travels well. Its qualities photograph clearly and are self-sufficient enough to hold their own when viewed out of context. Finally, operative periods of styles are the most distinguishable from each other and provide the most usable framework for general theories of art. It is clear, therefore, that the traditional predilection of scholarship for unity predisposes theoreticians to make certain value judgments that are not always recognized.

The scholarly attitude is thus in accord with that of those who would centralize control over a culture. Quite apart from its content, then, to the degree that a work of art can be seen to reflect a style, it functions as propaganda. At the moment that the work affirms, denies, questions, or in any way deals with attitudes common to its culture, it legitimizes these attitudes. The claim for the existence of styles, therefore, demonstrates an essential and unbreakable link between a work of art and its context, regardless of the content of the work. One may well question, therefore, works that claim for themselves purity, abstraction, and universality.

It is often believed that cultures are more productive during times of harmony. But those who held on to the Classical values of harmony, order, and repose must have been hard-pressed to do so during the 1930s when faced with the spectacle of authoritarian governments of the most ruthlessly repressive sort enjoying widespread approbation by their contented and productive citizens. Hierarchical modes of thought are given up only after great resistance to the contingent and discomfiting reality of modern life.

For, as has been shown previously, the Modern point of view is essentially inclusive and empirical. It has developed from a respect for data derived from observation, which has succeeded speculative Rationalism as the basis for generating knowledge. Purportedly universal values have given way in the face of objective consideration of equivalent cultural alternatives. Other cultures, other times are always under consideration for possible relevance to modern circumstances. Ironically, this desire to learn from the past comes about only after detachment from the myth of civilization has been achieved. To search sincerely for one's roots in past cultures such as those of ancient Greece and Rome is to discover much that is alien and strange. Restraint in judging such cultural differences is symptomatic of the acceptance of the ineluctable unknown, which manifests itself in Modern art in tones of violence, fear, and tragedy.

Thus, the influence of history is stronger than ever in the modern world. It is the *authority* of the past that has been tempered. The weight of historical fact has grown large enough to crush any naive faith in monolithic cultural values. The various empires of thought that were constructed before the nineteenth century had their foundations in a faith that masqueraded as knowledge. Today, faith is generally recognized to have been undermined in favor of the sort of belief that acknowledges alternate opinions about what is known. Absolutist hierarchies are threatened by a relativistic mode of thinking.

The manifestation of Modernism in art, then, calls for an entirely new approach to the problem of style. The great theories of cyclical development have failed, as Schapiro points out, to reconcile the overall patterns proposed with individual developments.

The normal motion and the motion due to supposedly perturbing factors belong to different worlds; the first is inherent in the morphology of styles, the second has a psychological or social origin. It is as if mechanics had two different sets of laws, one for irregular and another for regular motions; or one for the first and another for the second approximation, in dealing with the same phenomenon. Hence those who are most concerned with a unified approach to the study of art have split the history of style into two aspects which cannot be derived from each other or from some common principle.[47]

As it becomes more and more hopeless to fit the increasing mass of art historical data into simple stylistic theories, the nature of Modern art becomes more and more ineffable in the traditional conception of style. The three-part development of style mentioned earlier does not describe the movements in art since 1890 very well and certainly not at all in the cases of Wright and Le Corbusier. In the most fragmented manner, different movements have gone through various developments in different places at different times. Style in the old sense seems to be best understood if each individual artist is granted an individual style.

Certainly, a multiplicity of styles can be taken as typical, if not symptomatic, of Modern art. The problem for the artist is a kind of balancing act determined by his sense of poise. It is striking, particularly in the work of Wright and Le Corbusier, how the Modern artist always keeps revising his goals in his art. Even the finest, most finished works reveal the seeds of further development. Early goals are not so much abandoned as transformed, so that the sequence of work is always continuous. Where the greatest art of the past can be said to embody the quality of inevitability, the masterworks of Modern art tend rather to exhibit contingency. St. Peter's *sums up* the work of Michelangelo to that point in his career in a way different from what either the Guggenheim Museum or La Tourette does for its creator. This is not to deny their value as masterpieces of architecture, but only to point out that a hierarchical conception of style cannot take into account the contingency inherent in the content of Modern art.

Since the concept *style* is based upon the significance of that which is common to the works of different architects within similar cultural contexts, there can be no better foundation for a Modern formulation of style than the ground common to both Frank Lloyd Wright and Le Corbusier, as has been extensively explored already. It is in their work, more than in that of other architects, that one sees the first clear manifestation of Modern culture in architecture. And in spite of a hesitation on the part of critics to see them in the same light, no truly comprehensive assertion of Modern style can ignore either.

One turns, then, to the two ideas that have been proposed as the essential links between Wright's

Organic architecture and Le Corbusier's International Style phase. The first of these is dynamism, what has previously been defined as *the expression of growth, change, or movement*. It is directly opposed to the Classical values of harmony, order, and repose. A dynamic approach to style would focus on the *process* of the development of cultural values rather than on the values themselves. In this way, relativism is taken into account and judgment, in accord with fixed standards, is undermined. The influence of the past may be recognized, since even Classical values can be examined from the point of view of dynamism, but the authority of any value is to be questioned in the presence of alternatives.

The other idea linking Wright's work with Le Corbusier's is multiplicity. This has been defined as *the expression of interacting, independent systems* and denies the Classical values of unity, purity, and simplicity. A conception of style based on multiplicity would focus on the collision of competing values and would therefore judge from an inclusive point of view. Such a style would be concerned with the degree to which opposing values can be accommodated within cultural objects. This seems to be the view of Meyer Schapiro:

In modern literature both kinds of style, the rigorous and the free, coexist and express different viewpoints. It is possible to see the opposed parts as contributing elements in a whole that owes its character to the interplay and balance of contrasted qualities. But the notion of style has lost in that case the crystalline uniformity and simple correspondence of part to whole with which we began. The integration may be of a looser, more complex kind, operating with unlike parts.[48]

A conception of style derived from dynamism and multiplicity must also allow for the differences between Wright and Le Corbusier. But here, as Schapiro states, "the essential opposition is not of the natural and the geometric but of certain modes of composition of natural and geometric motives."[49] Important differences have been found in their chosen means of execution, in the development of functional prototypes, and in their attitudes toward nature. More particularly, the methods Wright used to execute his buildings were different among particular projects, relying on skilled labor and portable machine tools to adapt simple manufacturing techniques to field fabrication. Le Corbusier, on the other hand, counted on the development of sophisticated, mass-produced building systems, designed for general use, which could be combined in the field with a minimum of fuss. It is important, of course, to acknowledge that they both shared a dynamic consciousness of process and, with regard to multiplicity, both focused upon methods of assembling systems of building elements.

Wright developed a greater number of house types than Le Corbusier. But Wright's continual testing of new house types throughout his career is a natural result of his wish to adapt buildings specifically to their environments; Le Corbusier, on the other hand, tried to refine his own two house types so that their general applicability would be increased. All of this stems from their diverging attitudes toward nature, although each vastly enriched his work during his later career by adopting the earlier stance of the other: Wright became more generalized and less fussy in detailing and Le Corbusier worked with Organic principles as can be seen in his series of particularized churches.

These differences can probably be dealt with at the level of content rather than of style, for they deal with personal attitudes about common values rather than directly with the values themselves. As far as Modern style is concerned, for both men's work it can be defined as *a particular manifestation of interacting independent systems*. This definition incorporates multiplicity in that it demands that the work exhibit independently organized systems of building elements. Thus, where a Classical work is organized into a single hierarchy of large important parts and small unimportant parts, a Modern work will be composed of roughly equivalent systems of parts whose interaction cannot be predicted. Modern buildings reflect a balance of independent and conflicting values. From a dynamic point of view, the Modern definition of style calls for an interaction of these systems, a recognition of movement and change that is the essential Modern experience.

In avoiding a resolution of conflicting values, this definition abandons the old three-part stylistic cycle in favor of a continuing empirical and experimental avant-garde, a sort of critical wave just at the cutting edge of Modern theory that continually evaluates and questions developing ideas. Styles are not allowed to crystallize and become dominant; they are continually transformed into newer composites, a manifestation of the dynamism of the modern world. There is also an acknowledgment of the interaction between criticism and production of art, a quality especially pronounced in Modern art movements. Furthermore, with this definition there must be a multiplicity of styles in different stages of development at any given time.

When style is defined as a particular manifestation of interacting independent systems, it may include the Classical tradition as one of these systems. From the Modern point of view, the past is always a problem: The mixing up of facts, wishes, dreams, and beliefs that is characteristic of the Modern attitude toward history darkens the Classical tradition with the shadow of contingency. But even the mere denial of its authority, which has manifested itself in antiornamentalism, antiplasticity, anticolor, all of which

might be collectively termed antifrieze, is a response to the influence of the past. The forcing of crystallized styles through reductivist architecture cancels their Modern significance. The forms of the past are as meaningless as the supposed forms of the future so popular in *moderne* architecture. They may, however, be accommodated as a manifestation of a cultural system within the larger context of Modern style.

Before proceeding to the identification of particular styles in Wright and Le Corbusier, some mention should be made about the new importance of content, itself the subject of the next chapter. Meyer Schapiro mentions the problem of diffuse stylistic periods—such as the Modern—when different formal vocabularies can be observed in different fields of content.

It is such observations that have led students to modify the simple equation of style and the expressive values of a subject matter, according to which the style is the vehicle of the main meanings of the work of art. Instead, the meaning of content has been extended, and attention has been fixed on broader attitudes or on general ways of thinking and feeling, which are believed to shape a style. The style is then viewed as a concrete embodiment or projection of emotional dispositions and habits of thought common to the whole culture. The content as a parallel product of the same viewpoint will therefore often exhibit qualities and structures like those of the style.[50]

Therefore, an element of feeling or attitude—at what has previously been termed the poetic level—enters as content, impinging upon the manner in which conflicting cultural values are presented within a work of art. A democratic evaluation of cultural alternatives can be made at both intellectual and emotional levels and presented comprehensively through individual works. Values can thus be assembled into ideas and handled separately from stylistic operations. It is in this sense that Wright and Le Corbusier enter into a dialogue, exchanging different ideas about similar values through similar styles.

With the definition of style suggested above, several successive styles can be recognized throughout Wright's long career. His earliest and simplest thoroughly Modern style, termed Style I, is roughly equivalent to what has historically been called the Prairie style. Briefly reviewing what has been treated more extensively elsewhere in this study, one can define Style I according to clearly coordinated formal, functional, structural, and iconographic triads. Formally, horizontally attenuated and lightly hipped roofs stretch across a framework of ribbon windows, interrupted by massive walls and piers. Functionally, the masses screen the interior for privacy, the ribbon windows open out to nature, and the roofs lightly protect from weather. Structurally, the masses anchor the loads to the site while the wooden framework provides support for the glass beneath the cantilevered roofs. Iconographically, the wood-and-glass framework connotes a forest between the massive earth forms and cloudlike roofs while also displaying the cave within the tent. What is most important about Style I is that at every level the three opposed systems take on related meanings.

Style I is modified with the Usonian house to become Style I-A. The ribbon window system is expanded to take on a screen function through walls made of horizontally oriented boards. The hip roofs are simplified to wood planes. The four levels of interaction remain about the same, except that the brick masses have a more distinct functional role. The importance of the development is that the wooden roof slab is treated in a manner equivalent to the board walls, making manifest the notion of cloister prototype mentioned previously and beginning to break down the otherwise strict separation of analogous systems. This is also happening in the development of the red concrete floor slab, beginning as an earth system but taking on an abstract quality not derived from the general organization of the systems.

Style II can be traced through the wood-and-stucco Prairie houses and Unity Temple, but it becomes consciously present in the California houses of the twenties. Instead of structural systems clearly separated according to materials, the organization is based on the wall as a plastic medium, becoming either screen or support and sometimes sloped to express the screen function, as in the Ennis House. But the real opposition of systems occurs on a deeper level. Mass, whether screen or structure, is opposed to space as a second system and to circulation as a third. This three-part opposition can be clearly discerned at Hollyhock House and is developed fully in the Ennis House. In spite of the particularity of the materials, harking back to Style I, this is the basis for the organization of Fallingwater and the Johnson Wax Headquarters.

The most advanced of Wright's styles, Style III, is first encountered at Florida Southern College. The separation of materials, already diminished by Style II, is virtually obliterated, permitting an expression of essential substance. This generalized mass may be simple, strangely angular, profusely decorated: Such manifestations are no longer an issue at the highest level of systems. Space itself is treated as a sort of antimatter, an alternate condition for mass, but part of the same system. This can be sensed very strongly in the unusual canopied walkways at Florida Southern. The second system of Style III is circulation, sometimes demarcated as a path and sometimes no more than a carefully controlled sequence of spatial events. The third system is environmental, an open recognition of the influence of sun, earth, rain, and wind on the architectural continuum. Style III houses include the Friedman House, the Jester project, and all of the solar hemicycle type. In addition, most of Wright's late masterpieces, including the Guggenheim Museum, the Beth Sholom Synagogue, and the Marin County Civic Center, are examples of Style III.

The sequence of these three major styles indicates Wright's ever-growing mastery over the forces influencing architecture. Style I is simple, almost obvious. The programmatic alignment of the three systems at every level is characteristic of his experimenting with the coordination of independent systems. As he begins to realize the significance of his discovery, Wright reaches out for larger and more profound forces that influence his design, always organizing them into carefully poised, interacting systems. His final Style III achievement, then, in expressing substance, circulation, and environment as systems in opposition is no less than a profound disquisition on the collision of matter, man, and nature in the universe.

A similar stylistic breakdown can be derived from the work of Le Corbusier. Style I, the wall/window/roof continuum of strictly segregated material systems, is represented by the Catalan vault houses of his early and late periods. Wright's cruciform plan, generated in the Prairie houses by crossing two narrow bars of space, is replaced in the Catalan vault houses by a parallel alignment of narrow bars of space; the former reflects an openness to nature and the latter, a more protective attitude. The same style is thus adapted by each architect to assert his particular attitude about the circumstances of dwelling.

Le Corbusier's development of Style II—mass (as screen or structure)/space/circulation—is as gradual as Wright's. The studio-houses of the twenties, including the Villa Savoie, exhibit a development away from Style I and approach Style II in his late career. Termed Style I-B, this development begins with a simple and clear opposition of *piloti* structure, screen wall, and window systems, adding a fourth, circulation core, at the Villa Savoie. Le Corbusier's large-scale projects of the early 1930s offered him an opportunity to experiment with both Style I and Style I-B. The former can be discerned at the Pavillon Suisse, overtly in the ground-floor entrance unit and more subtly in the slab above, although the strict, parallel alignment of rooms is a direct translation of his Style I plan *parti* from the ground to the skyscraper. The studio-house style, Style I-B, is blown up at the Cité du Réfuge, where the spatial experiments of the entrance pavillons stand in contrast to the straightforward Cartesian slab behind. These come together at the Marseilles Unité d'Habitation as Style II. Although the strict material separation of Style I has been abandoned, the stark whiteness of Style I-B that emphasized the separation of structure and screen is also modified to a surface treatment emphasizing mass. In the broadest sense, then, Le Corbusier's development from the Catalan and studio prototypes through the two early skyscrapers to the mature Style II of the Unité is comparable to Wright's brick- and stucco-Prairie types that become, through the intermediate stage of the Barnsdall House and perhaps the Imperial Hotel, the mature Style II houses such as the Ennis.

Style III, where systems of substance/circulation/environment are placed in opposition, can be found developing through the *brises-soleil* of Le Corbusier's early skyscrapers. With the church at Ronchamp, Style III is given sudden overt life and becomes his major late style, no less dramatically than it did for

Wright. The churches, the Visual Arts Center at Harvard, and the buildings at Chandigarh are all essays in the expression of these counterpoised systems. The extremes of shadow and rendered surfaces of these works tend to sublimate all questions of form and construction to a most profound interplay of material and space. This system is balanced with circulation and with an organization of responses to environmental concerns such as daylighting, shading, and weather.

A case can be made, therefore, for the development of Modern styles as an excursion into ever-larger oppositions of universal systems. Evidence can be found in both Wright's and Le Corbusier's work for an empirical attitude toward the modern world, beginning with the establishment of dynamic opposition in what had been traditional building materials and becoming a recognition of the great independent forces of the universe whose circumstantial collisions produce the architectural continuum (figs. 9-1 a, b). Such a view recognizes the essential similarity between the two architects and provides for a comprehensive definition of Modernism while allowing for differences in attitude as expressed through architectural content.

This stylistic model also works from the viewpoint of iconography. Style I can be said to operate mostly on the *prosaic* level, accepting content that is matter-of-fact and easy to describe verbally and graphically. It is often characterized by highly articulated structural and formal systems. Style II operates between the *prosaic* and *poetic* levels, questioning the profundity of architectural issues. It is characterized by dramatic oppositions of mass and space and by emphasized circulation. Style III exists mostly at the *poetic* level, often accepting Style I and Style II manifestations as coordinated systems drawn at a smaller scale across the larger confrontation of material, movement,

and energy. Style III is sublime, ineffable; it speaks quietly of the enormous, slow-moving force systems of man's universe. The salvation of the poetic in Modern architecture, as called for in chapter 4, is achieved in Style III buildings. The mass/space conflict, emphasized by circulation, of Style II is trans-substantiated into a coexistence of matter and antimatter. The sharp distinction of inside and outside demonstrated by Wright's Style II Morris Gift Shop, for example, where an arched glass tunnel punctures a taut brick screen at the entrance, becomes a discourse on the degrees of *inside-ness* experienced at the entrance arch of the Marin County Civic Center. Instead of a brittle wall, one senses the gradual dissolution of the solid arched mass of the base up the side of the building into a loose fabric, woven on a circular warp at the eaves. In Le Corbusier's work, the opposition of the lifted block and entrance pavilion beneath, found at the Marseilles Unité (Style II), becomes a much gentler and more subtle interrelation at La Tourette (Style III). The ease with which space leaks through the semienclosed courts of La Tourette diffuses the opposition of mass and space so striking at Marseilles.

Most noteworthy of all is Wright's resolution of the cave and tent archetypes into a simple arc in elevation. At both the Marin County Civic Center and the Annunciation Orthodox church, there is an arched entrance into a mass crowned with a spherical or cylindrical vault, symbolizing in the simplest possible terms the cave beneath the tent. Similarly, in Le Corbusier's culminating masterpieces—La Tourette, the Assembly building at Chandigarh, and even the Zurich Pavilion—the fusion of tunneling and sheltering, of mass and screen, represents a similar resolution of the cave and tent. Based on the analysis made previously in this study, the same sort of resolution can be claimed for the cloister and shelter prototypes. The salvation of the poetic in Modern architecture, then, can be achieved through the clear manifestation of basic images as particularized spaces.

The three-level stylistic system provides a framework for comparing the work of Modern architects while maintaining an inclusive attitude. Not all architects are capable of working at Style II, even fewer at Style III. The system can be tested against the work of another of the major Modern architects, Alvar Aalto. It has already been mentioned that Aalto's work confirms the close relation between Wright and Le Corbusier by overtly incorporating ideas from both of their oeuvres. Perhaps the most startling example of this is Aalto's Maison Louis Carré in Bazoches, near Paris (1956–59). From the approach, the house reads as a Wrightian Prairie pavilion laid over a Corbusier studio-house. The plan has much of Wright's Usonian spatial flow, as well as his propensity for courtyards communicating with two residential wings forming an L. But it also has Le Corbusier's private bedroom-study suites, with views framed through white-painted walls. More than this, the quietly stated ambiguity of mass and space, the gently flowing circulation, and the subtle pitches and overhangs that respond to landscape and sky speak of Style III, and the house compares with Wright's Friedman House and Le Corbusier's Zurich Pavilion at this level. Moreover, the surface finishes, the structural elements, the lighting system, and the furniture are each handled as independent systems in the Style I manner.

Another of Aalto's buildings that seems to have a conscious mixture of Wright and Le Corbusier influences is the National Pensions Institute Headquarters in Helsinki (1952–56). From the park side, the complex nestles into its rocky site, its broad, low brick masses bringing to mind Johnson Wax, as does the low entrance to the top-lighted main

9-1a. Wright: Reisley House. Window detail.

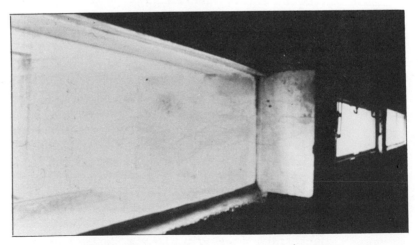

9-1b. Le Corbusier: Couvent de la Tourette. Window detail.

hall, overlooked by mezzanines. But the brick bands are stretched across what seems to be a curtain wall of complex rhythm. The narrowness of these bands and the complexity of the window grid result in an ambiguous reading between mass and volume. The Corbusier influence is strongest from the main entrance side, down the hill. Here, the brick masses are lifted on sturdy *pilotis* above the site. Again, the Style III opposition of material, circulation, and environment dictates the building's design, which is further instructed by Style I articulation of materials and finishes. The National Pensions Institute, then, can be compared with Wright's Marin County Civic Center and Le Corbusier's Secretariat at Chandigarh.

A final example in this vein would be Aalto's church at Vuoksenniska (1957–59). In spite of its white-rendered interior, the form of the church and its axial relations is reminiscent of Le Corbusier's churches at Ronchamp and La Tourette. The daylighting, above the first-floor level, is not unlike Wright's Annie Pfeiffer Chapel. Again, the direct and simple expression of substance, human movement, and daylighting as independent but interacting systems is a Style III manifestation.

Aalto goes further than either Wright or Le Corbusier in making tangible the ever-uncertain collision of universal systems. An Aalto plan after 1950 seems to catch a moment in time when the designer froze the interacting forces that generated the design. Aalto is the action painter to Wright's cubist sculpture and Le Corbusier's collages. He has a Wrightian sense of craftsmanly detailing and of landscape, but he maintains the Corbusier respect for independent structure, even if the columns and beams are pushed out of alignment by the forces of circulation and daylighting. Working mostly as a Style III Modernist, Aalto handles formal and technical issues within the system of material as essential substance. Detailing

and finishes are handled directly, but with finesse. The intersection of lighting, ventilation, structural, and finish systems are revealed within the larger continuum of material, movement, and environment.

Aalto does not ordinarily deal with cave and tent archetypes as Wright and Le Corbusier do. He establishes instead functional prototypes for twentieth-century buildings and he derives these from particular interactions of the Style III systems. In his library prototype, the material subsystems are reticent. The functional system is based on a sequence from entry to main top-lighted reading area, with ancillary offices and rooms distributed along the circulation path. Clerestory windows and sculptured ceiling soffits capture daylight and bring it to the reading areas.

His churches also derive from a Style III source. The materials again are reticent, if richer than those in the libraries. Since the scale of the room is large, the structural subsystem is often emphasized. Functionally, the churches are organized as long, narrow wedges in which the seats focus on the severely detailed eastern end. The environmental system is more complex than that of the libraries in that it focuses daylight through special skylights on such features as the altar and font, in addition to providing even light through extensive clerestories.

Aalto's auditoriums display a rich interaction of subsystems at the level of material. Several structural systems—typically bearing walls, detached columns on a Cartesian grid, and radially oriented piers—intersect in plan. Columns and wall surfaces are often covered with rich materials such as marble and ceramic tile. Ceiling systems incorporating lighting, ventilating, and acoustic systems, all in sublime conflict, are carefully detailed. Within the functional system, the complex arrangement of entrance, arrival, ticketing, garment storage, and crowd distribution is made manifest as if according to the principles of hydrodynamic flow. The wide fan of the auditorium itself relates not to daylighting, usually, but to the act of focusing upon the stage. This denial of environmental influence is contradicted in the foyers and balconies outside the main hall, sensitively lit and oriented.

Aalto's office buildings are usually rich in finishes and simple in mechanical and structural systems at the material level. Functionally, they continue to resemble the Johnson Wax Headquarters in their multistory, top-lighted halls that are overlooked by mezzanines. Individual offices and corridors are handled in a straightforward way; there is no attempt at drama. Environmental systems are more pronounced in an urban sense: e.g., the window surrounds and operating sashes, the marquees and portes cocheres, the entrances and ground-level circulation appointments.

One of his latest-developing prototypes was for an apartment house. In its final form, the materials are again reticent, the stoutness of the walls responding to cold climates. Functionally, the plan is a fan shape, minimizing corridor lengths from the elevators at the apex and spreading toward the southern sun. The complex curve of the southern wall tries to maximize views and privacy. The living units would be identical except for their distortion by the environmental system.

Alvar Aalto, then, when evaluated according to a Modern concept of style, is seen to have been working at the most profound architectural level, what has been called Style III. The widely admired quietness of his forms and structure and richness of his finishes are a result of dealing with these concerns at a human scale within the larger system of material. There are no melodramatic spaces in Aalto's work; for him, the ineffable nature of matter and space calls for delicacy, a surrender to all of the competing claims for attention of the perceptive senses. His tactile wall surfaces and solidly framed windows turn away from the hierarchical orders of the past and face instead a world that is conscious of matter and antimatter. In the age of relativity, the issue of matter itself is as problematic as those of motion and of energy, related by Einstein as $E = mc^2$. These, then, are the systems that come together at the most profound level of Modern thought: matter/motion/energy, which manifest themselves in architecture as material/circulation/environment.

There have been many twentieth-century architects who reject the Modern point of view. For them, dynamism and multiplicity represent a devaluation of universal ideals. They are disturbed by the contingency of Modern forces and seek to avoid it through reason and intellect. They attempt to identify universal values and build their art upon a more or less reasoned structure of principles. Such an approach is symptomatic of a twentieth-century strain of Neoclassicism, an attempt to update, in a circumstantial way, the ancient tenets of harmony, order, and repose. Architecture of this type has nothing to do with the stylistic development described heretofore: Judgment of such work must be based, as it always has been, on the validity of the primary assumptions and the lucidity of the concomitant stylistic manipulations. The most brilliant Neoclassicist of twentieth-century architecture was Ludwig Mies van der Rohe. He is mentioned here in contrast to Wright, Le Corbusier, and Aalto, for his artistic aims could not be more different from theirs.

The most advanced Modern style—what here has been termed Style III—is generated from the interaction of three independent forces directing the design of a building: material, movement, and environment. Mies's style, on the other hand, depends on the subjection of function to a hierarchy derived from a strict combination of form and structure. He reduced building programs to two functional prototypes: the Cartesian office building and the glass pavilion. Although Mies used similar building systems to construct both types, they really have very little to do with each other in any way but the superficial. One does not generate the other in the way that Le Corbusier's Catalan vault house generates his apartment buildings. It is highly symptomatic of modern reality that Mies was unable to find *one* functional prototype: The Neoclassicists of the eighteenth century did quite well at deriving almost everything they needed from a basic Classical temple.

The elegance of Mies's style and the influence that it has had on contemporary Neoclassicism is testimony to the reverence with which the past is still seen in the twentieth century. Sober and graceful, his lucid structures conjure up once again the dreams of simplicity and perfection that have haunted Western man since the ancient Greeks. The clarity of his details, achieved only at great expense, is enough in itself to convince anyone who has not actually experienced contemporary construction practice that design is an act of purest reason. Mies offered in his buildings a confirmation of order and hierarchy, which was extremely popular among the institutions and businesses that were his clients. It is interesting that the impact of his city skyscrapers—most particularly in the Seagram Building in New York—depended a great deal on their contrast with their messier neighbors. When Seagram carved itself a space out of the unbroken building wall along Park Avenue, it was a thing of rare presence. Now that it has been neighbored by sloppier versions of itself, much has been lost.

For the past remains in the Modern era only as a sort of dream of itself. There are alternatives today to Neoclassicism that have at least as much validity. Mies's dilemma is not in the exquisite logic of his form and structure nor even really in his first principles, for they, after all, are identical with those of Ictinus, Bramante, and Schinckel. It is the value of those principles, no longer confirmed by the larger culture, that has been lost. The roar of conviction has become a cry of despair. Even this, as profound matter for architectural content, is not special to Neoclassicism; Le Corbusier evokes the loss of the past perhaps even more tragically in his later buildings, as will be discussed in the next chapter. Neoclassicism exists today for those who shun the complexity of modern life, who seek to avoid the great increases in scale at all levels, who fear the contingent. In contrast to Modern style, then, *a Neoclassical style is a particular interpretation of value within a hierarchically ordered Classical system.*

In sum, it has been shown that a definition of Modern style can be derived from an analysis of the works of Wright and Le Corbusier. Such a definition acknowledges the close similarity between their oeuvres and can be used to evaluate the work of such other Modern architects as Aalto. It clearly distinguishes itself from the Neoclassical style of Mies van der Rohe. What remains to be done, finally, is to take account of the differences between Wright and Le Corbusier as spokesmen for opposing ideas about the effect of Modern forces upon the individual. Between them, they cover a vast range of expressive potential, from optimism to pessimism, from humor to tragedy. Furthermore, it is the profundity of their vision, expressed simultaneously on many levels, that awards them credence as partners in defining a relevant Modernism. This is the essence of content in Modern architecture, the subject of the next chapter.

10 Wright and Le Corbusier as Partners:
Content from the Inclusive Point of View

It has been useful in the preceding discussion of Modern style to maintain the traditional assumption of architecture as a branch of the fine arts. This is, after all, the way architectural theory and criticism has developed and it is reflected in libraries, bookstores, museums, and, in many cases, educational institutions. In the history of styles, the link has held up well even into the Modern era, with developments in the fine arts usually being quite clearly matched in stylistic terms with associated movements in architecture. Of course, the hierarchical nature of Classical and other traditional systems of thought—from medieval scholasticism right through the Age of Reason—must be taken into account as a compulsion toward unifying such potentially discrete cultural manifestations. But in stylistic terms at least, the marriage seems to have been fruitful.

When one considers the nature of the content of a work of architecture, however, this traditional link does not work as well. In the first place, it is only fairly recently—with the growth of serious architectural criticism beginning in the late nineteenth century—that such considerations have even begun to be made. Historically, the content, or subject matter,

of architecture was taken rather for granted. If money and time were to be spent on a building project, it was expected that some claim to prestige or amenity (or both) would be apparent in the result, and that this would include an evocation of renowned works of architecture from the past. In other words, architecture was only about itself.

There is an important distinction to be made here between architecture and the representational arts—painting, sculpture, literature, and drama. For them, the propriety of subject matter and the treatment of thematic material has always been an issue both overt and understandable. It is interesting that experiments in the representational arts during the Modern era have sought to reduce the content until the work was about itself alone, while in architecture theorists have generally tried to expand the range of content of buildings. Architecture is in some ways more like music; there is something pure and direct about its subject matter that is far more easily perceived than written about.

That there is in fact such a thing as architectural content, however, is certainly beyond doubt. One characteristic of the Modern era, exemplified by

Wright and Le Corbusier, is that its architects practice with a unique self-consciousness—thanks to the wealth of contemporary criticism and theoretical writings in regard to the meaning behind their work. Considering the degree to which the Modern attitude is an empirical one, it is useful to look at science for possible illumination on architectural content. After all, much of the actual practice of architecture is technical in the scientific sense.

It has traditionally been held that the sciences are different in kind from the arts. The goal of science is to discover a repeatable result that is therefore true. The goal of art is to discover a unique result that is therefore true. Architecture successfully practiced appears to incorporate both goals simultaneously. While there is a continuing demand for the perfecting of building types, there is a concomitant requirement for the particularization of each building to suit its site and its use. As a result, where the representational arts have been seen to have the culture as the source for subject matter, architecture itself is the subject matter for culture, the representational manifestation of the social beliefs of its time. To the extent, then, that science partakes of cultural involvement, architecture is the representation of science as well. For instance, the formulation of Einstein's theories of relativity had to wait until the proper experiments could be made. The data had always been available, but the culture determines what questions may be asked, and these questions are not restricted to science alone. It is in fact characteristic of Modern culture that equivalent truths are sought from different sources.

The separation of style and content, then, enables architecture to be seen as a representation by a culture of its values. First of all, a work of architecture is a record of its own process of creation. As such, it becomes an assessment of human culture in the larger natural world. It can be a measure of man's self-esteem. More specifically, a work of architecture is a representation of a particular place. And finally, it may be a statement of individual importance for the architect, the owner, the builder, or—best of all—the user.

In this sense, style can be seen as the record of a discussion among architects, whereas content is the manifestation of an agreement between the architect and the user. The user contributes to the meaning of a work of architecture by investing his consciousness in it. It is this particular aspect of the style/content duality that has become important in Modern architecture. The level of participation demanded of the user is new; it represents the importance of individual consciousness in the Modern world, analogous to the democratic issue in politics. As manifested in works of architecture, it can be recognized in the fragmented quality of Modern buildings and in the importance given to circulation as a system.

In making demands upon the user, architecture acknowledges the empiricism of Modern thinking. Although Modern science was founded upon the principles of experimentation and scientific method developed by Rationalist philosophers, today's scientists no longer speak about constructing great theoretical edifices. Stephen Jay Gould, biologist and geologist, characteristically writes:

Scientific discovery is not a one-way transfer of information from unambiguous nature to minds that are always open. It is a reciprocal interaction between a multifarious and confusing nature and a mind sufficiently receptive (as many are not) to extract a weak but sensible pattern from the prevailing noise.[51]

Or Marvin Minsky, mathematician and cofounder of the Artificial Intelligence Group:

Right now, I am working on the society-of-the-mind theory. I believe that the way to understand intelligence is to have some parts of the mind that know certain things, and other parts of the mind that know things about the first part. If you want to learn something, the most important thing to know is which part of your mind is good at learning that kind of thing. I am not looking so much for a unified general theory. I am looking for an administrative theory of how the mind can have enough parts and know enough about each of them to solve all the problems it confronts.[52]

This last quotation indicates the dissolution of traditional barriers between artistic and scientific thought. Differences in modes of thinking are accepted empirically as characteristics of human consciousness, not as intrinsic qualities of knowledge itself. Minsky's biographer has written:

Minsky and [his associate] Papert began to try to invent [computer] programs that were not centralized but had parts—heterarchies—that were semi-independent but could call on one another for assistance. Eventually, they developed these notions into something they called the society-of-mind theory, in which they conjectured that intelligence emerges from the interactions of many small systems operating within an evolving administrative structure.[53]

Minsky and others working in this field believe that in time the functional parts of the brain will be identified and their function described in language we can understand. Still, these people seem certain that the description, whatever it turns out to be, will not be like the great unifying descriptions in physics, in which a single equation, or a few equations, derived from what appear to be almost self-evident principles, can describe and predict vast realms of phenomena.[54]

Such is the essence of Modern empiricism. Thought and knowledge themselves are subject to scientific investigation in new fields such as information theory. Noted mathematician Leon Brillouin, a leader in this field, has written:

[Science] represents a logical summary of human knowledge, based on human observation and experience, both of which are always of limited range and finite accuracy. As for the logic introduced into the classification of empirical facts, it is typically a product of our brain. We select experimental results that appear to us as logically connected together, and we ignore many facts that do not fit into our "logic." This rather artificial procedure is our own invention and we are so proud of it that we insist its results should be considered as "laws of nature."[55]

Modern thought, then, has at its core a profoundly new conception of knowledge, one that, although it has been taking place for at least a century, is only recently beginning to be recognized by writers. Brillouin elucidates:

During the past few centuries, philosophers took a traditional approach to scientific problems. They assumed theoretical geometry to represent perfect scientific knowledge, with mechanics approaching perfection and physics not very far from it. This childish pattern cannot be maintained nowadays and we must emphasize the fundamental structural difference between mathematics and physical (or chemical and biological) theories.[56]

The content of Modern thought generally is characterized by determinants quite different from those of Classicism. *Contingency* has been mentioned before in this connection, and it should not be surprising to discover that it is an important concept in Modern science.

. . . an infinite amount of information can never be obtained. An infinitely small distance cannot be measured. Geometrical and mathematical definitions are only dreams which the physicist cannot trust, and we should especially emphasize the impossibility of physically defining a continuum in space and time. . . . No physical object can display real geometrical properties to the limit assumed by mathematicians; we may even call it "wishful thinking."[57]

In this regard, doubt becomes intrinsic to the scientific method and manifests itself in the open, independent systems of the architecture of Wright and Le Corbusier. Contingency, the element of the unknown, can be represented with fear and tragedy, as in Le Corbusier's late works, or with power and strength, as in Wright's work.

This brings up another determinant of Modern thought, *relativity*. The decline of absolute systems has initiated a search for new standards of value. "In the inanimate world, we confuse scarcity with value; what is exceptional is remarkable; the improbable, the unusual, is admirable. This confusion would be inadmissible in morals, in philosophy, or in criminology."[58] A concomitant of empirical attitudes is utilitarianism, an empirical approach to value. In this sense, judgment itself has become devalued. One no longer has clear choices between good or bad, but looks instead for that which works, that which is relevant or that which is real; different selections may result in each case.

Any observation (we have learned by experience) represents a perturbation, and influences the course of facts. . . . The study of the "coupling" between the observer and the observed system, between man and physics, will probably oblige us to revise the notion of value and to dissociate it from that of scarcity, but this step has not yet been clarified.[59]

The most apparent manifestation of relativity in art and architecture has been self-consciousness, that element which recognizes the contribution of an observer.

A final determinant for Modern thought is *intellectualism*. Such ideas as have been presented here are hard to understand at the scale of everyday reality, even though they are pervasive at the larger scale at which major cultural determinants operate. It is the situation of modern individuals to feel detached from experience at the same time that more of their attention than ever before is demanded by the powerful cultural forces at work in the modern world. The Modern situation can perhaps best be described as a sort of diffusion of self, a condition of alienation familiar to students of existentialist thought.

In order to deal with all this at the architectural level, it will be best to propose a model for Modernist thinking, using a theory particularly representative of contemporary concerns. This is the theory of *entropy*, based on a concept from the physical science of thermodynamics but extended by Leon Brillouin to information theory and thus to theoretical physics and mathematics. It is pertinent because it deals with the essence of empiricism: the effect of observation upon a physical system. Brillouin writes:

This picture of an objective real world around us is what we have inherited from the Greeks, and we must get rid of it. . . . We cannot abstract ourselves from the world. We form, together with it, an unseparable whole. . . . philosophers of our time cannot ignore the fact that interaction between observer and observed is finite and cannot be made as small as desired. Observation and perturbation inevitably go together, and the world around us is in a perpetual flux, because we observe it.[60]

The theory of entropy has been used in the analysis of contemporary literature[61] and will be developed here for the potential of its assistance in understanding Modern architecture.

Although the amount of energy in any closed thermodynamic system (such as the universe) is believed to be constant, it exists in different grades. Nuclear and electric energy are considered high grade; chemical energy, middle grade; and mechanical energy, low grade. High-grade energy tends to decay toward low-grade energy and this tendency is called *entropy*. It might be said that highly discrete or particularized forms of energy—with high potential for use—degrades toward complete homogeneity— and uselessness. By analogy, if not example, a photograph depends for its clarity on the degree of contrast between the dots or grains of black and a white field. The less contrast, the less information is transmitted, until the same amount of ink, evenly distributed, produces a homogeneous gray, totally without informational value. In this sense, the theory of entropy holds that it is the nature of the universe to approach uniformity. "For any isolated system, the total energy remains a constant, but the total entropy has a tendency to increase."[62]

But this tendency can be reversed by being observed. Information about a closed system increases its potential usefulness. Consider a system consisting of a quantity of iron, a quantity of coal, some water, and a potential heat source, such as a match. By itself, this system cannot perform useful work. But information about the substances involved, obtained through observation of the system, enables a steam boiler to be built from the components. Entropy has been reversed; work is done by the system. In this way, observation of even minor differences between elements of a system enables those elements to be combined in a way that produces useful work. This is more than just philosophical speculation. The concept of entropy has been supported by experimental observations at the microscopic and macrocosmic dimensions; it is associated with the basic theories underlying modern quantum mechanics and advanced physics, such as the Heisenberg uncertainty principle.

Even in this highly simplified description of entropy, ideas that have been proposed earlier in this study as key to the Modern way of thinking can be identified. The notion of continual change, of the degrading of the quality of energy, is at its core dynamic. Likewise, to reverse the direction of the closed system by outside observation is to acknowledge multiplicity, the interaction of independent systems. The dynamic interaction of building systems in Modern architecture, then, is related to the thermodynamic theory of entropy through its representation in architecture of an idea characteristic of its culture. For science is no less characteristic of its culture than art, and it is not unreasonable to propose that whatever cultural forces influenced Modern scientists to develop the theory of entropy must also have influenced Modern architects in their thinking. After all, today art and science are seen to have as a common goal the establishment of connections between human consciousness and a contingent universe.

The Modern view of consciousness, then, can be derived from the entropy model.

Any additional information [*decreases the entropy*] *of the system.* . . . *We may define a quantitative measure of the information by the corresponding* [*decrease of the entropy*]. *The additional information, obtained at a given moment, will progressively lose its value, for the system, abandoned to itself, naturally evolves toward more probable states of* [*more entropy*].[63]

This is an affective view of consciousness, very different from the model of an idealized, detached observer proposed by Rationalist science. It tends to interpret consciousness *as a system,* interacting with, and modifying, if only for a time, a physical system. "Acquisition of information about a physical system corresponds to a lower state of entropy for this system. Low entropy implies an unstable situation that will sooner or later follow its normal evolution toward stability and high entropy."[64] Such a view can ultimately incorporate consciousness itself into theoretical propositions derived from observation.

Entropy is usually described as measuring the amount of disorder in a physical system. A more precise statement is that *entropy measures the lack of information* about the actual structure of the system.[65]

Any system on which information has been recorded will deteriorate in the course of time.[66]

It will quickly be perceived that the Modern notion of incorporating the effect of the observer into the observation is diametrically opposed to the Classical view of a detached, speculating observer. And when architects engage the observer in their works, leaving parts of the puzzle out for him to supply, they are dealing with content in a particularly Modern way. This is the key that opens the door to the salvation of the poetic. While acknowledging the ineffable quality of architecture, that element of contingency that does not ever resolve itself, the Modern architect still insists upon the connection of man's consciousness with nature. The rejection of hierarchical order replaces the dream of complete knowledge with the unceasing desire to learn.

In opposition to the Classical point of view, which saw nature as a complete and perfect closed system over which man would gradually but inevitably increase domination, the entropy model offers an ambivalent interpretation. Entropy increases, but in-

formation reverses this tendency. Since time degrades the value of the information, it must be constantly renewed to be effective in controlling entropy. It is the particular value given to each of these elements that differentiates the content of the work of one Modern architect from that of another. Wright and Le Corbusier can be seen as examples of this.

Le Corbusier represents a view that accepts the degrading process—the approach of randomness, entropy—as finally more powerful than the information/observation counterprocess. Such a view can be discerned not only in each of the stylistic levels—I, II, and III—that characterize his work, but also in the development of the three styles as well. In a late Style I building, such as the Cité du Réfuge in Paris, the systems represented by wall/window/structure are all composites of regular geometric shapes. These shapes—squares, rectangles, and circles and the solids generated from them—can be totally defined mathematically. In this sense, they carry the highest degree of information; it is only in their assemblage, the contingent interaction of independent systems, that the information is degraded. Entropy has been expressed acting on the Classical hierarchy, fracturing its perfect shapes and releasing its components. It is represented more strongly in the Pavillon Suisse at the Cité Universitaire; here, the glass wall consists of ambiguously alternating bays rather than the strictly repetitive units of the Cité du Réfuge. Also, the square windows on the rear facade are separated by different intervals; they are perfectly determined shapes at indeterminate locations. More evidence of increasing indeterminacy lies in the composite piers that hold up the slab, the free-form entrance pavilion beneath and the gray color of both smooth and rough masonry wall surfaces.

In the Style II Unité d'Habitation at Marseilles,

all these elements have become less defined, more contingent. Even the famous *béton brut* is achieved by imperfectly filling the forms. Two stages of decay are embodied in *béton brut*. First, the simple geometry that determines the overall shape of the form is degraded by lining it with rough timber. Second, the concrete mix itself is stiff; it leaves the form with surface bubbles, leaks, and discolorations that are the marks of independent physical processes whose action has compromised the goal of filling a perfectly determined void.

At La Tourette and Chandigarh, quintessential Style III works, the preceding traits have been expanded again by large-scale tears and bends of the fabric of the buildings. Strongly differentiated window systems are used; environmentally related funnels, reflectors, spouts, and umbrellas are stuck on all over; free-form poured concrete walls express a gestural response to the interactions of the material, circulation, and environmental systems.

Thus, the tragic nature of these late works, so often commented upon, stems finally from the surrender of the architecture to the contingent forces of nature. The remorseless pressure of entropy is barely slowed by the intervention of man. This is a European view, a sensibility most strongly attuned to the loss of perfect order. There is heartbreak in the desperate splashes of bright color that try in vain to cover the indeterminate surfaces of raw concrete.

Frank Lloyd Wright, on the contrary, can be seen to represent the triumph of information over entropy. His Style I Prairie houses, as seen along the streets of suburban Oak Park, make a clearer statement of function and geometry than their neighbors, while remaining open to further development. It is the strength with which Wright defines his systems and the conviction in the detailing of joints that determine

the optimism so apparent in Organic architecture. Wright's cavelike masonry masses, unlike the burial caverns of Le Corbusier, are typically provided with a fireplace at their cores and so embody the possibility of man's protection from natural forces.

With the Style II buildings—such as Johnson Wax and the Morris Gift Shop in San Francisco—the loose rectangles and flattened prisms of the Prairie style are replaced by simpler, more determinate geometric shapes such as hexagons, squares, and circles. The profusion of moldings and decorative detail is constrained within sharply defined borders and the joints between systems are even more simple and direct. Yet, the dynamic quality of entropy is represented by the collision of shapes, indeterminate in their variations.

Style III for Wright is characterized by a primary interest in the most determinate of geometric shapes, the circle. Plans based on the intersection of circles appear in houses, the Guggenheim Museum, the Marin County Civic Center, and many other late buildings; the circle for Wright was the ultimate statement of dynamism. His cones, drums, and spirals explore the range of dynamic growth and delight in collisions between material, circulation, and environmental systems. Even the noncircular buildings such as Beth Sholom Synagogue are developed as studies in crystalline growth.

Frank Lloyd Wright, then, sees as triumphant the power of discovery over the constant flux of natural forces. The dynamism of nature is for him a tendency to grow. His typically American belief in increasing prosperity is in stark contrast to the European fear of poverty, expressed in their preoccupation with minimal environments. He invests man with energy, with the ability to control social as well as natural forces. The bubbly decoration on many of his late works—the Marin County Civic Center, the Greek

Orthodox church in Milwaukee, the Guggenheim Museum—expresses the effervescence of the eternal optimist. Thus the range of Modern content, as exemplified by Wright and Le Corbusier, is extremely broad and allows for subtle and precise expression of particular attitudes.

Today, the need for critical interpretation is stronger than ever. Modern modes of thinking are not yet easily accessible to culture, if in fact they will ever be. It has been shown here that to accept, as one inevitably must, the connection between the work of Wright and Le Corbusier is to surrender totally those Classical attitudes toward knowledge, toward art, and toward culture itself that hinder an accepting vision of dynamism and multiplicity. By giving up hope for a complete theory, one may achieve a comprehensive theory. By giving up the quest for unity, one may achieve clarity.

Notes

1. Christian Norberg-Schulz, *Intentions in Architecture* (Cambridge, Mass.: MIT Press, 1965), 7.
2. Robert Venturi, "Nonstraightforward Architecture: A Gentle Manifesto" in *Complexity and Contradiction in Architecture* (New York: The Museum of Modern Art, 1966), 16.
3. Attributed to Le Corbusier by Theo van der Wijdeveld, quoted by Nikolaus Pevsner in *Architects' Journal* (4 May 1939), 732.
4. Henry-Russell Hitchcock and Philip Johnson, *The International Style* (New York: W. W. Norton, 1932, rev. ed. 1966), vii.
5. Sigfried Giedion, *Space, Time and Architecture,* 5th ed. (Cambridge, Mass.: Harvard University Press, 1967), liv.
6. Peter Blake, *The Master Builders* (New York: W. W. Norton, 1976), 7.
7. André Wogenscky, "Foreword" in *The Open Hand: Essays on Le Corbusier,* ed. Russell Walden (Cambridge, Mass.: The MIT Press: 1977), xi.
8. E. Baldwin Smith, "Preface" in *Modern Architecture: Being the Kahn Lectures for 1930* Frank Lloyd Wright (Princeton: Princeton University Press, 1931), 6.
9. Museum of Modern Art, *Catalogue for Modern Architecture: International Exhibition* (New York: The Museum of Modern Art, 1932).
10. Frank Lloyd Wright, "Towards A New Architecture," *World Unity* (September 1928), 393. I am indebted to Robert Twombly's extensively researched biography of Wright for bringing this reference to light.
11. Museum of Modern Art, op. cit., 12ff.
12. Ibid., 18ff.
13. Ibid., 77.
14. Ibid., 75.
15. Ibid., 22.
16. Ibid., 37.
17. Frank Lloyd Wright, *An Autobiography* (New York: Horizon Press, 1977), 341.
18. Ibid., 342ff.
19. Museum of Modern Art, op. cit., 29.
20. Le Corbusier, *Towards a New Architecture,* trans. Frederick Etchells (New York: Holt, Rinehart & Winston, 1960), 123.
21. Ibid., 128.
22. Frank Lloyd Wright, *In the Cause of Architecture* (New York: Architectural Record Books, 1975.) Originally published in *Architectural Record.*
23. Ibid., 169.
24. Ibid., 168ff.
25. Museum of Modern Art, op. cit., 16–17.
26. Charles-Edouard Jeanneret (Le Corbusier), *Oeuvre Complète de 1929–1934,* 8th ed. (Zurich: Les editions d'architecture, 1967), 13.
27. *Zodiac 5* (Fall 1959) 28 (translation).
28. Olgivanna Lloyd Wright, *Our House* (New York: Horizon Press, 1959), 45.

29. Giedion, op. cit., 873ff.
30. See note 10.
31. Wright, *Autobiography,* 361–74.
32. Ibid., 363.
33. Ibid., 368.
34. Ibid., 373.
35. Ibid., 374.
36. Reyner Banham, *Theory and Design in the First Machine Age,* 2nd ed. (New York: Praeger Publishers, 1967), 363ff.
37. Vincent Scully, *Frank Lloyd Wright* (New York: George Braziller, Inc., 1960), 13–14.
38. Hitchcock and Johnson, op. cit., 13.
39. Charles Jencks, *The Language of Post-Modern Architecture* (New York: Rizzoli International Publications, Inc., 1977), 7.
40. Norris Kelly Smith, *Frank Lloyd Wright: A Study in Architectural Content* (Watkins Glen, N.Y.: The American Life Foundation, 1979), 153ff.
41. Colin Rowe and Paul Slutzky, "Transparency, Literal and Phenomenal," in *Perspecta 8;* ed. Jonathan Barnett and Michael Dobbins (New Haven: Yale University School of Architecture, 1964), 45–54.
42. Barry Maitland, "The Grid" in *Oppositions 15/16: Le Corbusier 1905–1933;* ed. Kenneth Frampton (Cambridge, Mass.: The MIT Press, 1979).
43. Manfredo Tafuri, *Theories and History of Architecture;* trans. Giorgio Verrecchia (New York: Harper & Row, 1980).
44. Peter Collins, *Changing Ideals in Modern Architecture, 1750–1950* (Montreal, McGill University Press, 1967), 216, 282.
45. Meyer Schapiro, "Style," in *International Symposium on Anthropology, New York, 1952: Anthropology Today*, A. L. Kroeber, Chairman (Chicago: University of Chicago Press, 1953), 294.
46. Ibid., 295.
47. Ibid., 299.
48. Ibid., 293.
49. Ibid., 300.
50. Ibid., 305.
51. Stephen Jay Gould, "This View of Life: Agassiz in the Galapagos," *Natural History* 90 (December 1981), 14.
52. Quoted by Jeremy Bernstein in "Profiles: Marvin Minsky," *The New Yorker* (December 14, 1981), 126.
53. Ibid., 118.
54. Ibid., 121.
55. Leon Brillouin, *Scientific Uncertainty and Information* (New York: Academic Press, 1964), vii.
56. Ibid., 33.
57. Ibid., 35.
58. Ibid., 9.
59. Ibid., 10.
60. Ibid., 52.
61. See Edward Mendelsohn, "The Sacred, the Profane and *The Crying of Lot 49,*" in *Pynchon: A Collection of Critical Essays,* ed. Edward Mendelsohn (Englewood Cliffs, N.J.: Prentice-Hall, 1978). Novelist Thomas Pynchon, whose work is the focus of this collection, is an outstanding exemplar of an overt treatment of the theme of entropy in literature. See also Joseph W. Slade's " 'Entropy' and Other Calamities" in the same collection (69ff).
62. Brillouin, op. cit., 6.
63. Ibid., 11.
64. Leon Brillouin, *Science and Information Theory,* 2nd ed. (New York: Academic Press, 1962), 159.
65. Ibid., 160.
66. Ibid., 264.

Selected Bibliography

Aalto, Alvar. *Alvar Aalto: Volume I 1922–62.* Zurich: Artemis, 1970.

———. *Alvar Aalto: 1963–70.* New York: Praeger Publishers, 1971.

———. *Alvar Aalto: Volume III Projects and Final Buildings.* Zurich: Artemis, 1978.

Banham, Reyner. *Theory and Design in the First Machine Age,* 2nd ed. New York: Praeger Publishers, 1967.

Benevolo, Leonardo. *History of Modern Architecture.* Translated by H. J. Landry, Cambridge, Mass.: The MIT Press, 1971.

Blake, Peter. *The Master Builders.* New York: W. W. Norton, 1976.

Brillouin, Leon. *Science and Information Theory,* 2nd ed. New York: Academic Press, 1962.

———. *Scientific Uncertainty and Information.* New York: Academic Press, 1964.

Brooks, H. Allen. "Frank Lloyd Wright and the Destruction of the Box." *Journal of the Society of Architectural Historians,* 38, no. 1 (March 1979): 7ff.

Collins, Peter. *Changing Ideals in Modern Architecture, 1750–1950.* Montreal: McGill University Press, 1967.

Dunster, David, ed. *Architectural Monographs 4: Alvar Aalto.* New York: Rizzoli International Publications, Inc., 1979.

Frampton, Kenneth. *Modern Architecture: A Critical History.* London: Thames & Hudson, 1980.

Giedion, Sigfried. *Space, Time and Architecture,* 5th ed. Cambridge, Mass.: Harvard University Press, 1967.

Gropius, Walter. *The New Architecture and the Bauhaus.* Translated by P. Morton Shand. Cambridge, Mass.: The MIT Press, 1965.

Hitchcock, Henry-Russell. *Architecture: Nineteenth and Twentieth Centuries,* 4th ed. New York: Penguin Books, 1977.

———. *In the Nature of Materials: the Buildings of Frank Lloyd Wright, 1887–1941.* 1942. Reprint. New York: Da Capo Press, 1973.

Hitchcock, Henry-Russell and Philip Johnson. *The International Style.* New York: W. W. Norton, 1932 (rev. ed. 1966).

Hitchcock, Henry-Russell and Philip Johnson, eds. *Modern Architecture: International Exhibition.* The Museum of Modern Art, New York, 1932.

Jeanneret, Charles-Edouard (Le Corbusier). *Modulor 1 and 2,* 2 vols. Cambridge, Mass.: The MIT Press, 1968.

———. *Oeuvre Complète de 1910–1929,* 9th ed. Zurich: Les editions d'architecture, 1967.

———. *Oeuvre Complète de 1929–1934,* 8th ed. Zurich: Les editions d'architecture, 1967.

———. *Oeuvre Complète de 1934–1938,* 8th ed. Zurich: Les editions d'architecture, 1967.

———. *Oeuvre Complète de 1938–1946,* 6th ed. Zurich: Les editions d'architecture, 1971.

————. *Oeuvre Complète de 1946–1952,* 6th ed. Zurich: Les editions d'architecture, 1970.

————. *Oeuvre Complète de 1952–1957,* 5th ed. Zurich: Les editions d'architecture, 1970.

————. *Oeuvre Complète de 1957–1965.* Zurich: Les editions d'architecture, 1965.

————. *Le Corbusier: The Last Works.* Zurich: Les editions d'architecture, 1970.

————. *Towards a New Architecture.* Translated by Frederick Etchells. New York: Holt, Rinehart & Winston, 1960.

Jencks, Charles. *The Language of Post-Modern Architecture.* New York: Rizzoli International Publications, Inc., 1977.

————, *Le Corbusier and the Tragic View of Architecture,* Cambridge, Mass.: Harvard University Press, 1976.

Maitland, Barry, "The Grid," in *Oppositions 15/16: Le Corbusier 1905–1933.* Edited by Kenneth Frampton. Cambridge, Mass.: The MIT Press, 1979.

von Moos, Stanislaus. *Le Corbusier: Elements of a Synthesis.* Cambridge, Mass.: The MIT Press, 1979.

Norberg-Schulz, Christian. *Intentions in Architecture.* Cambridge, Mass.: The MIT Press, 1968.

Rowe, Colin, and Slutzky, Paul. "Transparency, Literal and Phenomenal." In *Perspecta 8.* Edited by Jonathan Barnett and Michael Dobbins. New Haven: Yale University School of Architecture, 1964.

Schapiro, Meyer. "On Style." *International Symposium on Anthropology, New York, 1952: Anthropology Today.* A. L. Kroeber, Chairman. Chicago: University of Chicago Press, 1953.

Scully, Vincent. *Frank Lloyd Wright.* New York: George Braziller, 1960.

Smith, Norris Kelly. *Frank Lloyd Wright: A Study in Architectural Content.* Watkins Glen, N.Y.: The American Life Foundation, 1979.

Tafuri, Manfredo. *Theories and History of Architecture.* Translated by Giorgio Verrecchia. New York: Harper & Row, 1980.

Twombly, Robert C. *Frank Lloyd Wright: an Interpretive Biography.* New York: Harper & Row, 1973.

Venturi, Robert. *Complexity and Contradiction in Architecture.* New York: The Museum of Modern Art, 1966 (2nd ed. 1977).

Venturi, Robert, and Brown, Denise Scott. *Learning from Las Vegas.* Cambridge, Mass.: The MIT Press, 1977.

Walden, Russell, ed. *The Open Hand: Essays on Le Corbusier.* Cambridge, Mass.: The MIT Press, 1977.
    Wogenscky, André. "Foreword."
    Turner, Paul. "Romanticism, Rationalism, and the Domino System."
    Jencks, Charles. "Le Corbusier on the Tightrope of Functionalism."

Wright, Frank Lloyd. *An Autobiography.* New York: Horizon Press, 1977.

————. *In the Cause of Architecture.* New York: Architectural Record Books, 1975.

————. *Modern Architecture: Being the Kahn Lectures for 1930.* Princeton: Princeton University Press, 1931.

Index

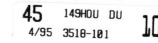

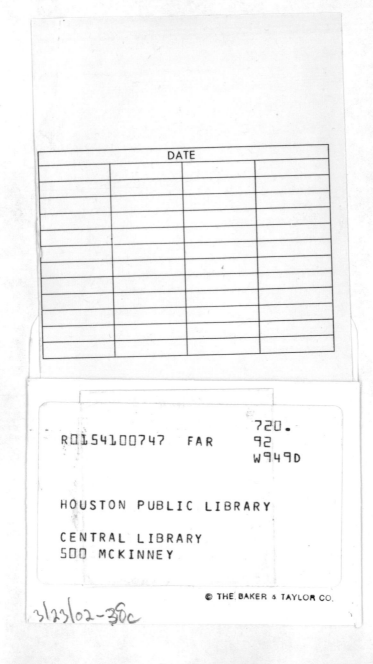